6/16/11

JANIE,

You were born

To SWEPED & GRACED

WITH A PURPOSE!

JUST KEEP PADDLING...

NOT TODAY SHARK!

One Salesman's Journey of Spiritual Growth

CAREY LOWE

Quantity sales special discounts are available on quantity purchases by corporations, associations, and others. For details, contact the publisher at the address above.

Orders by U.S. trade bookstores and wholesalers. Email info@ BeyondPublishing.net

The Beyond Publishing Speakers Bureau can bring authors to your live event. For more information or to book an event contact the Beyond Publishing Speakers Bureau speak@BeyondPublishing.net

The Author can be reached directly at BeyondPublishing.net

Manufactured and printed in the United States of America distributed globally by BeyondPublishing.net

BEYOND
PUBLISHING

New York | Los Angeles | London | Sydney

ISBN Softcover: 978-1-637920-22-0

ISBN Hardcover: 978-1-637920-51-0

Dedicated to Danea, my reason for reason.

"Showing others who suffer how we were given help is the very thing which makes life seem so worth while to us now. Cling to the thought that, in God's hands, the dark past is the greatest possession you have—the key to life and happiness for others. With it you can avert death and misery for them."
— ALCOHOLICS ANONYMOUS, p. 124

"Mother, mother ocean, after all the years I've found…
My occupational hazard being, my occupation's just not around.
I feel like I've drowned, gonna head uptown…"

Jimmy Buffett – A Pirate Looks At Forty

TABLE OF CONTENTS

PREFACE

The Tibetan word for meditation is gom. It simply translates to mean "get familiar with". For the last 61 years I've been trying to get familiar with this guy named Carey Lowe. Who is he? Where did he come from? Where is he going? Why is he here? What does he believe in? What legacy will he leave when he's gone? Without knowing it when I attended my first Alcoholics Anonymous meeting 20 years ago, I started down a path of spiritual growth that I still happily trudge along daily. At times this growth has been extremely painful and at others it has produced some of the happiest days of my life. In this book I hope to share some of the experience, strength and hope I have acquired along that path with you. I have had a slew of odd jobs here and there over the years but only two jobs that I would actually consider careers. My time in the U. S. Coast Guard and sales. As my military days are now behind me and I look proudly at that time as a valuable life lesson, my sales career is still very active. As I write this, I remember my very first sales job. I was about eight years old and living with my family in a suburban neighborhood of Thousand Oaks, California. I saw an ad in a magazine that convinced me I could get rich selling greeting cards door to door! Now, I really had no concept of what "rich" meant. All I knew was that I wanted to earn enough money to go to Disneyland. With my mom's blessing and help I ordered the sales kit and soon found myself walking around our neighborhood knocking on doors. Well, someone else must've seen that ad and beat me to it, because no one I asked was interested in buying any cards from me. Disappointed, I returned home with my box of samples and unfilled order blanks.

I asked my mom why wouldn't they buy from me. She in turn asked me, why would they? She then opened the kitchen drawer and showed me all of the greeting cards she had bought and never used. There were Christmas cards and Valentine's Day cards and birthday cards. She went on to explain that probably everybody whose door I knocked on had a drawer in the kitchen just like this one. She asked me what it was I told the people about my cards that made them any different than the ones they already had. I told her that I just showed them the samples and the low price and thought that was enough. She then asked me what I now know to be a 'disruptive' question. "Carey, why are you selling the cards?" Well, so I can go to Disneyland, I answered. Why don't you just tell them that and see what happens. I did. I sold them all. What I learned that day was the value of being transparent. In sales especially, people buy you before they buy the product. The more transparent you can be the better off and more successful you will be. But before you can be transparent, you must first get familiar with who you really are.

Carey Lowe

INTRODUCTION

The goal of this book is self-improvement. I was once told that you can't give away something you don't already have. If I could give any one gift to the people I love, it would be the gift of happiness. In order for me to give that gift away I have to first be happy myself. I was taught a very basic concept years back and now hold that concept as a mantra. You must first be before you can do and you must do before you can have and most importantly, you must have before you can give. While that may sound a bit confusing, it simply breaks down to mean, that if you think you can find happiness by having all of the things in life you want, you will be very disappointed. These things you have accumulated, will not last and very soon you will find yourself, once again, unhappy. The key to happiness then is to be happy, do the next right thing and you will, in turn have everything you've ever wanted. I was taught that I can have anything in life I want as long as I help enough other people get what they want. My purpose in life is to help as many other people as possible, get what they want!

The stories and techniques that I will share with you in this book are the tools that I use on a daily basis to be happy. My purpose for writing them down and sharing them with you is to simply reinforce them in my own head. So, in fact my reason for writing this book is quite selfish. The purpose of this book is self-improvement. My self-improvement...because I can't give away something that I don't have.

Chapter One

NOT TODAY SHARK…!

A few years back, I entered a paddleboard race. Not just any paddleboard race, The Hennessey World Championship Paddleboard Race.

Now for those of you who may be reading this from your inland living room, and have no clue what a paddleboard is, let me explain.

Surfing came to the world via the Hawaiian Kings who prone paddled their long koa wood surfboards in races to prove their superior waterman skills. In modern times we have replaced the heavy koa wood with carbon fiber, and prone paddling for the easier stand-up version, but we still race to prove our waterman skills!

I started surfing at the age of 12 in San Diego, California. Today, I consider myself an accomplished waterman. I have surfed waves all over the world; from two-foot waves in Ocean Beach, California, to overhead monsters in Hawaii. I now live in Baja California Sur, Mexico, and have for over three decades.

When I heard the Hennessey World Paddleboard Championships were coming to my hometown, I was genuinely excited! The fact that the event was honoring my longtime friend, the legendary waterman Mike Doyle, made it that much better!

The race was to be 18 kilometers or approximately 11 miles of open ocean from Punta Gorda to Punta Palmilla. No one even questioned my intention to enter the race.

You see, to my close friends and family I'm known as "Papalowe". It's become more than a nickname. It's actually become a responsibility.

I was a professional skateboarder in the 1970s and retired with a medical discharge from the US Coast Guard in the late 80s. We moved to Cabo San Lucas, Mexico, when my boys Kane and Kai were just babies.

The Lowe brothers (or Los Hermanos Lowe, as they are affectionately called in Cabo!) have been the state BMX Champions, the state Motocross Champions, and the state Surfing Champions. I have raced off-road for years. The Lowe boys are in it to win it!

However, The Hennessey World Championship Paddleboard Race would take some serious preparation. I started a regime of physical training specific to the type of conditions I would be encountering. I did hours of work in the gym with pulley machines that replicated the action of paddling; hundreds and hundreds of repetitions - 11 miles is a long way!

I had made the decision to paddle the race in the traditional (much more difficult) "prone," or lying down position. To further add to the fun, I borrowed one of Mike Doyle's vintage, hand-shaped paddleboards!

As the race date grew closer, I felt confident in my ability and in my level of preparation. Then, just two weeks before the race, I came down with a lower respiratory infection. My many years of off-road racing and inhaling dust had caught up with me. I found myself having to use a nebulizer just to get through the night. There was no chance of continuing my training. No way could I see to make it happen.

It was the evening before the race and all of the best watermen in the world were gathering at Palmilla Beach for the opening ceremony. On my way down to watch I noticed some of my buddies loading their paddleboards onto a truck at the surf shop, so I decided to stop and chat. They told me that all of the boards for the race had to be loaded up that night and driven out to the race start at Punta Gorda in the morning. If I wanted, they still had a spot for mine.

I had all but given up on the idea. After all, who would fault me in my condition? But the competitor awakened inside of me and I thought "Oh, what the heck!" Before I knew it I was driving home to get my board!

Race day I was surrounded by the best of the best; young and not so young, men and women, stand-up and prone. I was entered in the over 50/stock 12´/prone class.

Then I heard it, "You aren't really gonna paddle that in the race…are ya'?"

These guys all had state-of-the-art carbon fiber boards that had been specially designed for THIS race! My "vintage" Doyle weighed at least 10 times more than what surrounded me on that beach.

We got our final race instructions; beach start, paddle out one-half mile around the buoy and then head downwind the remaining ten and a half miles to Palmilla Beach. The race official said they expected the winner to do it in about an hour and a half but were allowing three hours for the race.

GO!!!!!!

They started the pros first and then the rest of us 30 seconds back. Since I was prone-paddling, my strategy was to hang back at the start (so I didn´t get hit in the head with a paddle) and catch up after the turn.

Bad strategy!

The light boards being maneuvered from the stand-up position became natural sailboats when they rounded the buoy and headed downwind! Within five minutes I was in last place and couldn´t even see the guy in front of me.

Oh yeah, and I was still sick.

The excitement and adrenaline caused my bronchial muscles to spasm. I couldn't breathe. So, I just sat there straddling my board one-half mile out to sea. I thought of the relief I could get from my inhaler, if I only had it!

No!

I scolded myself. I´d have to dig a little deeper into my tool box to get through this one. Luckily, I had accumulated A LOT of tools!

Now, understandably for some people, sitting alone, having a bronchial attack, one-half mile from shore (and a deserted shore at that), might take them past their comfort zone straight into their "danger zone"!

But, I'm a waterman.

I've probably spent as much of my life in the water as others spend on land. Being in the water is my safe place, my church, my sanctuary. So, there I sat. I really don't know how much time had passed before the spasms subsided, but when I looked up, I saw that one of the race committee boats had been sent back to pick me up. He asked me if I was alright and told me that it was ok if I got in. No shame. A lot of people start this thing and don't make it.

Give up? Not an option. Remember, I'm Papalowe!

Since Kane and Kai paddled out through the surf to take their first waves, raced their first bicycle race, experienced their first Baja 1000 from the pits, battled through lap after grueling lap of motocross, I had made one important concept clear to them; to finish first, you must first finish!

No! I would not quit.

I waved away the rescue boat, put my head down, and started paddling. After about a half hour of good paddling I thought I was making steady progress. Surely, I was catching up to the pack.

Now, let me take a minute to describe my surroundings. The tip of Baja, California, is rugged landscape. A 7,000-foot mountain peak known as the Sierra la Laguna towers over the desert as its base slips into the Sea of Cortez. Some 39 million years ago, massive shifting of the San Andreas Fault caused the mighty Sierra Mountains to split, creating Baja, California, and the Pacific Ocean filled in the gorge.

Punta Gorda, our starting spot for the race, stuck out from the land, so by now I was quite a ways offshore in very deep water. From my low vantage point on the water I could not see my destination, but my many years as a navigator in the US Coast Guard taught me to triangulate my position. That is to take two points of reference on land and draw a triangle back to me. I knew if I did this and kept moving, I could track my progress.

I took notice of the landscape of the shoreline and the mountain peaks behind them, and kept padding, and paddling, and paddling.

Just keep paddling…

I prodded myself. I had no idea of actual time as I had decided not to wear a watch that would cause extra drag in the water.

The race had started early but I could not deny that the sun was full in the sky. The glare on the water was intense. I had on plenty of sunscreen. My sunglasses and hat were comfortable and I was really thankful for my last- minute decision the day before to spend $75 on a backpack hydration system!

Just keep paddling…

I could tell I was getting into deeper water because it became increasingly more difficult to keep my board straight as the groundswells beneath me started to pick up my board and send it sideways.

Though I was honored to be riding a Mike Doyle Classic board, it was not designed for the conditions I was facing, or my body size. I am about 6 feet tall and weigh 185 pounds.

The board was custom made for a 5'5" woman who barely weighed 100 pounds! As the ocean swells increased it became impossible to get the board to glide. The preferred race technique is to take four or five strong strokes and then glide for about 20 to 30 feet to rest. The only way to keep my board straight was to keep padding. If I stopped, the board slid sideways and it stopped. No glide, no rest. No bueno.

Just keep paddling…

I had to dig deep. The heat was starting to take its toll. The dried saltwater on my sunglasses made it hard to see.

Just keep paddling…

Prior to my getting sick, I had put in substantial time in the gym. Not lifting traditional weights, but creating exercises that work the muscle groups I would need to call on today. One particular exercise had me sitting on a Pilates ball with a 30-pound weighted pulley behind me. As I brought the cable down to the floor it replicated the motion of a full paddle stroke. I did thousands of strokes with my eyes closed; picturing myself on the board, picturing the water, picturing the glide, picturing the finish line.

From the horizon I could see a committee boat! I knew I must be approaching the pack! As it drew closer, I realized my folly. It was the head lifeguard of the race; a mountain of a man that knew his stuff when it came to water safety. He had come to insist that I get in the boat! He said I had been paddling for over three hours and wasn´t even half-way there. Even if I could keep up my pace it would be another three hours.

The race is over, dude. Get in the boat.

I was confused. My triangulation skills were thrown off by the distance to the mountain top I was using in relation to my position in the water. It all looked the same from where I was.

The head lifeguard told me that the race had been won by a guy from Australia on an 18 ft. custom carbon board. It was the same guy that had commented on my board earlier that morning!

Well, his race may have been over, but not mine!

I told the official I wasn't giving up and he didn't need to worry about my safety. He told me I was nuts and headed off into the horizon.

Well, now at least I knew how far I had gone, and I had a clear idea of how much farther I had to go.

Just keep paddling…

The sun was getting really hot. The waves were getting bigger and it grew increasingly harder to even stay on the board, let alone make it go anywhere.

Just keep paddling. Keep paddling.

Then something happened. The ocean took on an iridescent quality. It seemed to change colors as I paddled through it. I could actually feel the fish swimming beneath me. I felt as if I had become part of it, as opposed to being on it. I lost any conscious knowledge of the action of paddling or of the board beneath me.

That's when I saw…The SHARK!

Now I don´t really know, looking back on this, if I actually saw him or just felt him. Any surfer will tell you, you can "feel" the presence of a shark. The vibration of the water actually changes. This guy was BIG!

I took a quick look over my left shoulder and saw the disturbance of the water surface. I adjusted myself on my board, took five long, strong paddles and told him in no uncertain terms, "Not today shark, not today!"

By the time I could see the shoreline of Palmilla Point the sun was already low in the sky. The fishing boats in the bay were setting their anchors for their evening rest before taking the tourists out again in the morning. I was tired but I knew I could finish. A local fisherman told me the officials had been asked to radio the local boats to look for me. That felt really good to hear.

As I approached the shore, I felt a new strength inside me. I always told the boys how important winning was, but how much more important style was! I made sure my strokes were perfect.

What I saw next made me cry! I still had to run up the beach to the finish line. Even though the race had ended for everyone else hours ago, they had all stayed to see me finish. The kids made a "love tunnel" for me to run through. When I crossed the finish line the people who mattered most to me were there with the best hugs ever!

That night at the awards ceremony (I always taught Kane and Kai to go to the awards ceremony whether they won or not, out of respect for the race and its competitors) I was surrounded by my family. As they read off the awards, I couldn't believe my ears!

First place in the over 50 stock prone division - CAREY LOWE! It seemed the other guys in my division…did get in the boat.

Chapter Two

THE WALK ABOUT

I wasn't always that positive and self-motivated however...

Tom Ziglar, proud son of Zig Ziglar and president of Ziglar Inc. shared with me one of the secrets to his dad's success. He told me his dad had enjoyed speaking to crowds of thousands, and having personal audiences with presidents and celebrities, but it was not his speaking and motivational skills that got him there.

Tom explained that his dad´s inspiration came from a place of brokenness. That news resonated deeply and took my thoughts back in time.

One fine Mother's Day morning, in the year 2000, my sons helped me put the final touches on the 1972 Cadillac convertible we had restored. It had been purchased six months earlier; a rust-eaten, hard top, two-door, Eldorado.

Now, her top chopped, she was about to win first place in a car show!

How proud I was to be in downtown Cabo with my family on that beautiful day in May. Car shows are great family events and everybody seemed to be out, enjoying each other's company and looking at all of the magnificent entries.

My marriage had had its ups and downs and before I knew it, we were headed for an all-time low! Over the course of the day, I had way too many beers and on the way home we got into a huge fight that quickly escalated out of control.

By the time we got home, I was drunk and fit to be tied. I got violent and slapped her and when my youngest son tried to defend her, I slapped him, too. He went outside and starting beating on the Cadillac with a hammer.

After about ten minutes of me screaming, yelling and breaking things, I hopped into the Cadillac, fired it up and screeched out of the driveway.

Now this car was a beast. She had the 500 engine and was running great. I stood up hard on the gas pedal and the speedometer quickly passed the 100- mph mark. At that time, we lived on the top of a hill overlooking the ocean on the outskirts of town. Within five minutes I was clear of Cabo headed towards La Paz on Highway One.

I had no idea where I was going. I just wanted out! I purposely drove down the centerline divider; I didn't care what might happen. I screwed up. I hit my wife. I hit my kid. You just don´t do that! I knew it was over. My marriage, my family - everything!

I was so drunk that I didn't even notice the engine had quit because I had run out of gas. When I finally came to a stop, the Caddy was rammed into a fence about 50 feet off the side of the road, on the wrong side of the highway!

Sitting there in a drunken funk, I decided to try and tear the stereo out of the dashboard. Maybe I could sell it to someone. I pulled cables and ripped wires, eventually getting the power booster out instead. Booty in hand, I worked my way back to the highway.

I decided the best and only option I had was to get as far away as was possible from those I had hurt. I started walking right down the middle of the highway, just wishing that a bus would take me out. No such luck. I kept walking for about an hour with my thumb out hoping for a ride.

A tow truck pulled over and said he could take me as far as the next pueblito (town) about five kilometers down the road. I told him about the caddy on the side of the road and said if he wanted it he could have it. I gave him the power booster, too!

The rest of the night was spent walking and reflecting on what I had done. The mess I had made of my life, the two boys I felt I no longer had the right to hold, the job I would lose, the wreckage I was leaving in my wake. I wanted out so badly.

I caught a ride the last few miles from La Paz with someone who was even drunker than I had been earlier. My 95-kilometer walkabout had sobered me up pretty good, but that ride scared me to pieces! No problem, I wanted to die anyway.

Somehow, we made it to La Paz and I found a place to sleep on some cardboard under a pier. I was exhausted and totally beaten.

When I awoke the next morning, I felt even worse. I had 85 pesos (about seven dollars at the time) on me. As soon as I saw the Farmacia open, I went in and asked them to give me the strongest pain killers they had. I'm sure they noticed the unshaven, dirty condition I was in because they told me they wouldn't sell anything to me.

I found a Pacifico beer store and bought a Ballena instead. I went across the street to the beach and sat under a palapa where I drank the whole quart of beer in no time at all.

Ah, that was better!

I went back to the store and bought two more. Yeah…get numb… make it all go away.

At that moment I was truly in my comfort zone! I looked over on the beach and saw a length of baling wire. I laughed out loud, because my boys had always joked that you could repair anything with baling wire and in the Baja, you were never more than ten feet away from finding some! This baling wire would fix my problems for good.

I wrapped the wire around my neck as tight as I could and twisted it. I closed my eyes and drifted off to peace - and in that peace I found my mom! Mom had passed away fifteen years earlier; right after my youngest son Kai was born. But there she was, very alive! She told me I wasn´t done. That I still had work to do. Marriage or not, I still had two boys who depended on me.

Somehow, I woke up enough to unwrap the wire and I knew I had to go home. The scar on my neck is a daily reminder of how close I came to losing my life that day.

I started hitchhiking out of town and was picked up by an old Mexican man in a rundown van with no side door. He was obviously a carpenter; half-built chairs and cabinets filled the cabin. As I got out of his van, he told me not to worry, that God had a plan for me and that everything was going to be alright. I said "Gracias" and asked his name.

Jesus, he replied.

I got in touch with my boss back in Cabo, and he said everyone was worried sick and thought I had been kidnapped. The police found my caddy on the side of the road with the stereo ripped out and suspected foul play.

He sent his sister-in-law to get me. She appeared like an angel, bought me a torta (sandwich) and put me on the bus.

Another longtime friend and sales manager picked me up at the station in Cabo and let me take a bath at his house while he made me the best lambchops I had ever tasted. I was feeling very fortunate to have the friends I had!

Bob Beaudine, in his book The Power of Who, tells us to nourish our Inner Circle of 12-3-1 (twelve friends, three whom are very close and one who is considered our best friend). This becomes the base of our "Who." Our closest friends are our "Inner Circle" of greatest influence. I found out who two of my "Who" were that day.

My sales manager said that I needed to go see my family and he asked me to promise I would go to Alcoholics Anonymous.

I knew broken people went there.

Chapter Three

DO THE WORK!

I kept my promise and crawled into AA. On their advice, I attended 90 meetings in 90 days. I got a sponsor. I did the work.

Step 1. Honesty

Step 2. Hope

Step 3. Faith

Step 4. Courage

Step 5. Integrity

Step 6. Willingness

Step 7. Humility

Step 8. Brotherly love Step 9. Forgiveness

Step 10 Perseverance

Step 11. Spiritual awakening

Step 12. Service

Amazing things happen when you replace bad habits with good habits.

I continued working for the same company selling timeshare for the next 13 years. Once I quit spending half the day nursing a hangover, my productivity greatly improved.

I wrote over a million dollars a year in business for the next 11 years straight, setting the company record for consistency. Now, I feel it's important to note, what I wasn't doing. I wasn't breaking any sales volume records, I was breaking sales consistency records. Persistent consistency. To me, this has been my secret of success. When I was first introduced to the time share industry in 1998, I had already had a successful foundation in sales. After leaving active duty in the U.S. Coast Guard, I returned to Southern California and settled in Newport Beach, Ca. Feeling like I had no actual sellable skills other than being a legal pirate, (the U.S. Coast Guard can board any boat without a warrant and confiscate what they find, then seize or if necessary, scuttle the boat!), I found comfort living in a town surrounded by and basically dedicated to boating. My Coast Guard background would become my qualification to a long and prosperous sales career. After seeing a want ad in the paper for a sales position, I applied for a job at one of the many boat dealerships in the area. During my interview, it became glaringly obvious to the sales manager that I had no previous sales experience. He said this would actually work in my favor, as I also had no bad sales habits! He told me I had the one thing that would insure my success. A love of boats and the feeling you get when you are on one. Sales is a transference of feelings. He said that if I just stayed transparent and transferred those feeling to my clients, I would quickly rise to the top. He said my Coast Guard background was all the credibility I would need.

When I first enlisted in the Coast Guard and was about to head off to boot camp, my dad gave me the best advice I've ever been given. My dad was and will always be my hero. He had joined the marines at age 17 and was a tail gunner over Guadalcanal during WW2. He had an amazing career as a flight engineer for Pan American World Airways traveling all over the globe for over 33 years. Advise from my dad always came from a place of experience and worldliness. He explained to me, that in boot camp I was going to be tested.

Not only physically, but mentally as well. He went on to say, that they were going to teach me things that on face value, didn't seem to be important or even faintly related to the job I was preparing to do. Here's the advice he gave me, and the advice I would in turn, offer to anyone...

Always sit in the front row. When they ask for volunteers, raise your hand. When they are teaching you something, take notes. It doesn't matter if you think what they are teaching is important or not, learn it. Become the best at it. When it comes time for advancement, they won't be looking for the strongest, they will be looking for the one who can teach everyone else. My first day in boot camp, they asked for volunteers to join the Ceremonial Honor Guard. Of course, I raised my hand. That moment, set off a chain of privileges and advancements that have worked in my favor to this day.

By 1998 I had already lived in Los Cabos for about 5 years. I was successfully selling real estate to tourists wanting to escape the cold winter where they lived. The market for investment in Baja was perfect. It was a lot of hard work and time, however. Real estate transactions in Mexico are completely different than in the U.S. and closings can take up to a year. That's a long time between paychecks for a young father of growing boys. As luck would have it, I had a close friend in the timeshare business who suggested that I come work for him. He said, It's a lot easier to sell someone the two weeks they actually need in the beachfront condo, instead of convincing them the need to own and maintain all 52. Besides, we get paid every Friday! Having had no experience or training in this particular field of sales, but knowing that the best salesman in Los Cabos were working for that resort, I felt the move was the right one. It was. I sat in the front row at meetings. Something else happens when you do that. You end up sitting next to the best salesman on the team. I can guarantee, the best salesman is not hiding in the back of the room! I would look over his shoulder every morning and noticed he always had the same routine. A routine that I adopted and continue to this day. He always had a notebook and a pen ready for every morning meeting. At the top of the page he would put the day and date. Below that he would write the following; SPOM-SPOY (I would soon find out this meant, Salesperson of the month - Salesperson of the year.) Next to that he would write his sales volume goal for the year and below that his exact sales volume as of that morning. He would do the math and write down the difference. He would then divide that number by the number of days left in the year. Now, he knew exactly how much he had to sell today. He finished the routine every morning, by writing the affirmation, "I can, I will, I'm positive". He finished the year in first place, and was later promoted to assistant manager. Years later, when it was time for him to step down, I was chosen as his replacement.

My new lease on life had given me a second chance at being the best dad I could be. We surfed together, raced motocross together, traveled together and genuinely enjoyed being together. To this day, Kane and Kai are my best friends and I continue to grow prouder of them as they have become mature men and fathers themselves.

I was told once and believe that your legacy is better caught than taught.

A lot of growth happened during those years. As I participated actively with my boys through their motocross days, the values I was teaching them about teamwork, fair play, hard work, practice, playing through the pain, not giving up, maintaining your equipment, humility in winning times and grace in defeat, rubbed off on me. I could no longer just talk the talk, I had to walk the walk. Raising my boys taught me to lead by example.

As the years went by however, I learned there was a lot more to spiritual growth than just being sober.

Chapter Four

THE EDGE

When I first walked into an AA meeting, an old friend who was already sober asked me, Hey Carey, how close to the edge do you need to stand?

I was about to find out.

NOAA BULLETIN

HURRICANE RICK ADVISORY NUMBER 14 NWS TPC/ NATIONAL HURRICANE CENTER MON OCT 19 2009

INTERESTS IN SOUTHERN BAJA CALIFORNIA AND THE SOUTHWEST COAST OF MEXICO SHOULD MONITOR THE PROGRESS OF THIS EXTREMELY DANGEROUS CAT 4 HURRICANE. A HURRICANE WATCH MAY BE REQUIRED FOR PORTIONS OF SOUTHERN BAJA CALIFORNIA.

You could feel the electricity in the air. Every year, hurricane season in Cabo San Lucas keeps the population on the edge of their nerves. Hurricane Rick was sitting a few hundred miles off of the coast and had grown to a very dangerous category 4. From the window of my office on the Pacific side, I could see the massive ground swells rolling in from the south and giant plumes of whitewater smashing into the beaches and rocks a few hundred feet below. The interesting thing about a hurricane in the tropics (as opposed to let's say a snowstorm in the Northwest) is that they may or may not hit and until they do, the weather is gorgeous… it is the tropics after all!

So, even though there was the possibility of total mayhem sitting just off the coast, this Monday morning was like any other Monday morning. You get up shower, shave and go to work. As I pulled out of my driveway earlier that morning and started off on the 20-minute drive to work I could already see the perfect 10-foot waves rolling into my favorite surf spot. I slowed down to say 'hola' to some of my luckier buddies that didn't have to work that day.

They all asked me if I was going out. Understandably, paddling out in 10-foot hurricane surf may sound a little crazy, but having lived in the tropics as long as I had and having over 40 years of big wave surfing experience…The guys I was talking to had come to expect it from me. There's a core group of surfers that look forward to hurricanes as giant wave machines. A large hurricane, sitting a few hundred miles off the coast sends a perfect wave barreling towards the shore every time it makes a circulation. At certain points on the coast where the reef is far enough out, these waves could be ridden, no matter how large they got.

"Not right now" I told them, "I've got to go to work for just a little while but I should be back before the tide starts to drop, maybe around 1 o'clock…" "That sounds like a plan", they all said. The waves should be really good by then as the tide just begins to change. There's not any wind right now and it looks like it will be perfect conditions all day!"

At work I kept getting messages telling me that the conditions were getting bigger and better with every wave that rolled in. It became increasingly hard to keep my focus on my job, all I wanted to do was grab my board and get in the water! Included in that core group of big wave surfers are two of my favorites. My sons, Kane and Kai. We had moved to Los Cabos from Newport Beach California in 1992 when Kane was just 2 1/2 and Kai was only one.

They learned how to swim in the ocean before they could walk and grew into very experienced watermen. The two of them had earned a well-deserved reputation as being some of the best surfers in the area. My youngest son Kai was the one sending me the messages, as school had been canceled that day due to the impending storm. He had already surfed earlier that morning and was waiting impatiently for me to show up and go back out. Unfortunately, my oldest son Kane would have to sit this one out. He had injured his foot earlier that week in a wakeboarding accident.

It was a very slow day at the resort where I work. I was done and ready to go surfing by noon. I called my ex-wife and let her know I was going to come home, change into my surf trunks, grab my board and go surfing with Kai.

Well, it turns out she had another agenda for me. Kane's injured foot had been really bothering him and he wanted to go to the doctor to get it x- rayed. "OK, you take him to the doctor and get it x-rayed", I said.

She complained that she didn't like doing that sort of thing and insisted that I take him before I go. Now this is gonna sound really selfish, but I was positive his foot wasn't broken and I really wanted to get in the water! I came home, picked up Kane and begrudgingly took him to the doctor. After what seemed like an eternity in the waiting room, we finally got in to see the doctor, got his foot x-rayed (it turns out he did have a hairline fracture after all!) got him properly wrapped up, waited for another eternity for his prescription to be filled and finally headed home. I quickly changed, grabbed my big wave board, threw it in the truck and headed for the beach!

By the time I got to the beach, conditions had changed dramatically from earlier that morning. The cliff along the coast was lined with emergency equipment, ambulances, tourists and locals all gawking at the giant waves rolling into the shore. A rescue attempt was being made for somebody who had been apparently swept out to sea. The perfect 10-foot waves I had seen earlier that morning we're now much larger. Probably somewhere in the 20- foot range. The perfect tide I had hoped for was now an extremely low tide which meant the waves were breaking further out on an almost dry reef a half of a mile offshore. I saw one of my buddies from earlier that morning looking exhausted, holding his broken board. It takes a lot to break a surfboard, especially a big wave board. Surfers call their big wave boards "guns", or "rhino chasers". You need completely different equipment to surf these extremely powerful waves. A normal surfboard is typically less than 6 feet long, very light and maneuverable. A big wave gun is usually over 10 feet long and glassed heavier for strength. You could probably drive a car over a big wave gun without breaking it. Seeing my buddy holding his in two pieces gave me an idea of the critical conditions in the water. "How was it out there?" I asked. "I don't know, I never made it out, my board got snapped by a big set before I could make it outside!" Well, I had brought my triple stringer gun built specifically for huge surf. This board could handle it. I headed down the steps to the beach where my son Kai had been waiting. He had been surfing all day! He told me the conditions were epic, but had been considerable better earlier when the tide wasn't so low as the rip currents weren't as strong. No worries, he was ready to jump right back in the water, but as I looked out at the giant surf, I felt an uncomfortable feeling that I wasn't used to.

As I mentioned earlier, the ocean is my sanctuary. My place of refuge and serenity. I was first introduced to surfing at the age of 12 when my family moved to San Diego, California. From the first day that I dragged my old, beat up 11-foot longboard into the sloppy waves of Ocean Beach, I was hooked. I quickly learned to sail and scuba dive. I have spent countless hours on, in or under the ocean. That passion led me to a career in the U.S. Coast Guard. I am trained and fully qualified to handle a rescue in just about any conditions the sea can whip up. That being said, the strength and unpredictability of the ocean is something nobody should ever take for granted. It will win.

I have learned, that most fear comes from a lack of preparation. Either physical or mental. My confidence in the ocean comes from many years of experience. I don't believe I've ever felt afraid to paddle out in any situation. No matter the condition of the ocean, it always seems to bring me a calm, serene feeling...Why was I feeling uncomfortable now?

Standing there on the beach with my son, all I could think about was my perception of my ex-wife being so inconsiderate! Why couldn't she have taken him to the doctor so that I could've gotten to the beach earlier? These thoughts grew into anger as the two of us spent the next 30 minutes battling through the rolling mountains of whitewater trying to get to where the waves were breaking outside. Realizing we were caught in the dangerously strong rip current and our efforts to continue were futile, we decided to head back to the beach and re-group. By then the conditions had all but made it impossible for anyone who wasn't an expert to be in grave danger. We could hear the rescue vehicle sirens from the highway above. Kai suggested we enter the water up the beach a few hundred yards. His local knowledge and experience at this particular surf spot made him just such an expert. He knew if we could successfully navigate the rocks, the rip current could work in our favor. Without hesitation I followed his lead. Now my thoughts had taken me to my older son, Kane. He's been hurt before, why couldn't he wait another day to go to the doctor? Was he just jealous that we got to go surfing and he didn't? Looking back, Those thoughts alone should have raised a huge red flag, as Kane is one of the most thoughtful, caring people I know! The paddle out this time was a success and the rip current took us right out to where the largest waves were peaking. By this time there was only one guy left out in the water. When we got to him, we could tell he was only out there because he couldn't get in! He was very scared and did not have the experience needed to stay out in these conditions. We gave him some valuable tips on how to get in and sent him to the beach. As I watched him belly-board in, my gut told me I should follow him. My ego said "paddle out!"

On a normal summer's day, the 2-3 foot waves at this spot break on the first reef just off the beach and it is a popular spot for tourists taking surf lessons. As the southern hemisphere swells from Australia arrive, 6 to 8-foot waves break off the second reef a few hundred feet further and only the expert surfers will paddle out. We were now on the outer edge of the third reef. A very shallow pinnacle of lava rock surrounded by very deep water. This is where the giant hurricane waves could be ridden. At a medium tide the conditions are perfect. The giant swells produced by the circulating hurricane travel through the deep water and are shot upward as they pass over the reef, producing a large fast rideable wall of surf. However, on an extreme low tide as it had become, the waves are much steeper and more dangerous to ride as it breaks over the almost dry reef. Kai was in perfect position as the first giant rolled in. He took three good strokes, quickly got to his feet made the drop, successfully navigated the bottom turn and kicked out of the wave as it exploded onto the reef. I thought I was in position for the next one as it approached. I turned and paddled for it but was just off the peak enough to miss it. This put me in a very bad spot as the rest of the set rolled in from outside. Kai was far enough out from his kick out on the previous wave to successfully make it over the top of all of the sets that came rolling in like an avalanche on a ski mountain. As I paddled with everything I had trying to make it over the wave that was coming at me, I realized I was in the worst possible spot. Directly in front of the dry reef. I made it about halfway up the wave as it fiercely broke in front of me. The impact slammed me off of my board and deep into the ocean. It's hard to describe the feeling of wiping out on a big wave and what happens to your body underwater... we call it getting rag-dolled. Picture a Raggedy Ann doll tumbling in the dryer. Head over heels, arms where your legs should be...legs were your arms should be   but you're

not in the warm dryer, you're 20 feet underwater and heading for the second reef. Instinctively you head for the surface. The problem is, after all of this tumbling around underwater, you are disoriented and have no idea where the surface actually is. With modern surfing came crowds. The surf leash was invented so that if you lost your board it didn't whack someone else in the head! On a big day you wear a leash for a different reason. It becomes your lifeline to the surface. I reached down to my ankle and found my leash. I then started climbing up to where I assumed my board would be floating on the surface. To my surprise when I reached my board, I was still 10 feet underwater. A surfboard as big and thick is the one I was riding is extremely buoyant, however the magnificent force of the wave that broke on me was holding it and me underwater. As I got close to grabbing it, the next wave broke pushing me and my board even deeper. I've wiped out on hundreds of waves. I've been held down multiple times. This one was different. I was scared. Once again tumbling underwater, out of control, knowing that the second reef must be getting very close. I also became aware for the first time that I was out of air. I no longer felt the pull of my surfboard above me. This meant one of two things, my leash had broken or my surfboard had broken.

Either situation, this far out on this big of a day could spell disaster. I've read a lot on the effects of adrenaline in stressful situations. It can give someone the power and strength they need to escape certain death. Using the adrenaline that my body had produced in reaction the extreme situation, I stroked with everything I had towards the surface. And then the third wave of the set broke! Still underwater, once again being rag-dolled toward the reef. The lack of oxygen to my brain was now starting to take its toll. The rush and subsequent crash of the adrenaline had left me completely out of energy. I was underwater, exhausted and could no longer hold my breath. I was experiencing something I had never physically experienced before. I was experiencing something however that I did remember from the book "The Perfect Storm". One particular paragraph describes how someone feels when they're drowning. "The instinct not to breathe underwater is so strong that it overcomes the agony of running out of air. No matter how desperate the drowning person is, he doesn't inhale until he's on the verge of losing consciousness. At that point there's so much carbon dioxide in the blood, and so little oxygen, that chemical sensors in the brain trigger an involuntary breath whether he's underwater or not...water floods the lungs and ends any waning transfer of oxygen to the blood. The clock is running down now;

half- conscious and enfeebled by oxygen depletion, the person is in no position to fight his way back up to the surface." I was aware of this. I knew not to take a breath. But I did. And as I did, I knew I was drowning. And going to die. They say your whole life passes before you before you die, for me it was just the events of that day. I realized that I never should've gotten in the water feeling the way I felt. I realized now...drowning, that I foolishly put myself into this position. However physically prepared I might have been...I was definitely not properly mentally prepared. My focus and concentration was off. Entering the ocean with the feelings of anger and resentment I was harboring literally almost killed me. It's been said that resentment is like taking poison and waiting for the other guy to die...now I truly believed it.

I've been told multiple times that I must have a guardian angel watching over me. Hearing Kai's Version of the story later, he told me he looked back over his shoulder as he paddled over that first set wave and saw me get pounded.

He said he waited for me to pop up but I never did. He then saw my board 'tombstoning', a term we use when a surfer's board is sticking straight up out of the water because the weight of the surfer's body on the leash is pulling the tail down. He knew I was underwater and needed to get to me. As the next wave broke he saw that it also broke my surfboard, and the front 2/3 of my board was washing towards the beach. He paddled towards the small piece of my board's tail that he could see, grabbed me and pulled me onto his board. I was able to take a life-saving breath of air and with his help, we made it to the beach together. It was getting dark. My friend on the cliff had seen the whole thing and said he knew I would be alright because Kai never took his eyes off of me. I felt the true meaning of grace that day.

The sirens we heard earlier paddling out were for a man that apparently hadn't been so blessed and had in fact, drowned.

Luckily, hurricane Rick fizzled out before making landfall. When we returned to work, I told the story of my near drowning to a close friend of mine. He said that I was a true inspiration and went around telling the story to everybody else. He was making me out to be an example of how you should never give up no matter what the situation was. However, I didn't feel that way about what had happened. To me, it was a wake-up call! It was God reminding me that even though I had quit drinking years before, the character defects that had brought me to my knees were still as healthy as my drinking habit had been years earlier. I would need to spend a lot more time and effort working on these character defects if I was ever going to live a life that was truly happy, joyous and free.

They say that hindsight is 20/20. I'm sure that is so because looking back it's glaringly apparent what my biggest character defect was, and in fact still is to this day.

I wish I could tell everybody reading this book that I had the cure. I don't. I don't know that anybody ever will. The key is identifying your character defects, understanding them and working on them daily in such a way that they cannot impede on your God-given birthright to succeed.

I used to think that it was my drinking that caused me to get angry and say things I wish I hadn't. I used to blame my drinking for getting me into all the trouble I was always getting into. But here I was years later, sober, still getting angry, still harboring resentments and still getting myself into trouble!

It became glaringly apparent, that we must constantly work to grow our spiritual self as well as our physical and financial self.

Chapter Five

WHAT WERE ONCE VICES...

So, what is that character defect that when left to his own devices is constantly holding me back? Is it possible that this one, character defect is the cause of all of my problems?

In 1974, I was in 10th grade. The Doobie Brothers released their hit album "What Were Once Vices Are Now Habits..."

Looking back, it's amazing that so many of the things I consider to be "the way I am" are habits that started that year. Some good. A lot of bad. I started skateboarding that year. I started surfing a lot more that year. I started smoking pot that year. I started drinking that year. I started feeling like I didn't fit in that year. I also joined Navy JROTC that year. A lifetime of daily decisions later, (the most powerful one was enlisting in the US Coast Guard), I still skateboard and surf, I don't drink or smoke. I have a lot of friends. The point is, we all make daily decisions to take action. Eventually, these actions become habits. We become slaves to these habits, good or bad. Now, it only makes sense that continued action based on bad habits can only lead to unhappiness. The opposite then is the answer. To be happy, we must make daily decisions to replace bad habits with good ones. One day at a time...one habit at a time. Is there a vice that has become a habit? Take action now!

Make a decision that today, just today...to replace that bad habit with a good one. If we make it through the day with the good habit, do it again tomorrow! It doesn't matter if we fall back into the vice, as long as we realize you are. Keep trying. The more bad habits we can replace with good ones, the more they become a pleasure to perform, and if it is a pleasure to perform, it is our nature to perform it often. We have to "prime the pump" in order to get water from the well. We have to put something in before we can get something out. It is so important then to guard what goes in.

The first step in identifying a character defect and its effects on your success is to recognize the trait as a bad habit that inhibits growth and separate it from your productive and growth producing character assets.

Some common character defects to consider might include,

Selfishness	Pessimism
Jealousy	Conceit
Arrogance	Stubbornness
Judging others	Defensiveness
Anger	Being overly critical of others or yourself
Cynicism	
Dishonesty with others or with yourself	Playing the victim
	Pride
Argumentativeness	Ego

A lot of us hang on to one or more of the traits listed above our entire lives. We feel "comfortable" with them and just go along saying "I've always been this way" or "my parents raised me this way". While we by no means need to be saints, we do need to recognize that over time our actions and reactions to situations usually stem from one or more of the items listed above.

How did we develop these traits? And when did they become a problem? If you were to analyze any one of these traits that we now recognize as a flaw in our character, we can go back to our childhood and see where it was developed. When we were children, we used this trait as a defense mechanism, it was there to protect us. But as time went on that trait became a habit and with all habits, we derive a certain sense of pleasure when we perform it. Whether the habit is healthy or not has nothing to do with the pleasure we derive from performing the habit. Take smoking as an example. When we were young, we started smoking so we would look cool. We did it so we could hang out with friends, but now 50 years later we realize smoking will kill us, and yet, some of us still derive pleasure from lighting up!

So, the one thing we know to be true is that if we want to change something, we need to take action. A lot of us spend our entire lives waiting for a higher power to fix our problems. While it's very important to realize that there is a higher power and that higher power has a plan for you and that plan is for you to succeed, we must realize that faith without works is dead. If we want to change something right away, we need to take action right away. For most of us these traits, that have now become habits have been with us all of our lives. Once something has become a habit you cannot simply stop doing it.

The only way to discontinue a bad habit is to replace it with a good one.

So, what good habit could replace a bad character defect? It's opposite...a character asset!

Let's take the first example of selfishness.

We must first acknowledge that we are being selfish. We must claim it as a defect that once had a place in our lives because of economic insecurity. Feel it, but don't feed it. In other words, it's alright to feel selfish and accept that you feel that way, but once you realize you are feeling something you don't want to feel...get rid of it!

To be rid of a bad habit we must replace it with a good one and to get rid of a character defect we must replace it with a character asset. In this case, that asset would best be, becoming charitable. By doing something as simple donating an old pair of shoes to Goodwill, or putting an extra dollar in the collection plate at church we can perform charity. If you make an effort to do at least one charitable act every day for the next 21 days it will become a habit. When something becomes a habit, it becomes a joy to perform and when something is a joy to perform, we will want to do it often and a good habit or character asset is born.

"LIFE IS ABOUT THE DECISIONS
WE MAKE EVERY DAY."

Carey Lowe

Chapter Six

SUCCEEDING VS. WINNING

It is very important before we attempt to dig any deeper into the causes and solutions to our problems that we define our purpose in doing so. Is it to make more money? Is it to get it a promotion at work? Is it to save your marriage? While all of these are very important goals, they should never be listed as our purpose. When we can honestly define our purpose as our desire to do God's will for us is when we truly open the door to spiritual growth. When we have complete faith that God's will for us is to be successful and that he has a plan for us to do so it makes it much easier for us to simply walk down the path God has laid in front of us. While God, is the ultimate power of the universe, he has endowed each one of us, individually with power nobody can ever take away from us. That is the power to control 3 things.

God has given us the power to control, The thoughts we think.

The images we project. The actions we take.

When we fully accept the concept that we are not in charge of the universe, that we are not in charge of how other people act, that we can only control the three things listed above we will find a certain serenity.

Most of us have been raised with the belief that in order for us to get what we want we need to win at the game of life. I'd like to attempt to change that paradigm.

The dictionary describes winning as achieving first position and/or getting a prize in a competition.

While winning may earn us a trophy, can it actually bring us happiness? Not necessarily. Many of us have sacrificed a great deal of happiness in our pursuit of winning. Now don't get me wrong there's nothing wrong with winning, there's just a problem with winning being your ultimate goal.

Let's dissect the concept of winning for a second. It has been said that failure is best defined as one's inability to reach a desired goal. If your goal is to win, and you didn't...then the result must be failure. We've all heard the phrase, 'second-place is the first loser!' Do you really think God put anything on this planet to lose? Do you really think God put anything on this planet to fail?

Even the smallest organisms are designed to grow and prosper. They have built-in defense mechanisms to help them succeed in their purpose.

Everything, no matter how small or large on this planet is there for a purpose.

Everything on this planet was born to succeed. And God has graced everything on this planet with a purpose. You were born to succeed and graced with a purpose!

So, I'd like to change the paradigm of being driven to win, which will inevitably lead to feelings of failure, to being driven to succeed, which eliminates the concept of failure.

So, What's the big difference between winning and succeeding? Well, winning is an absolute…you either win, or you don't. They may give awards for second and third place and you may get to stand on the podium next to the winner, but you didn't win! Don't get me wrong, I want every one of you to experience, many times in your life the thrill of standing on the podium and receiving the award for coming in first! The point I want to make is that winning shouldn't be your sole purpose. Your purpose should be to do God's will. God's will for you is to succeed. Can you fail at winning and still be considered a success? Of course! But if you consider success as your purpose, then you have to take the word fail out of the sentence! So, I didn't win but I'm still a success? Absolutely! Life is a journey, not a destination. Failure is an event, not a person. You didn't fail, you simply didn't come in first… this time!

Chapter Seven

CHANGING YOUR COMFORT ZONE PARADIGM

Have you ever had a dream where you were in school and you had to take a test, but you didn't study for it? Or how about the one where everybody has their homework except you. The one I used to have all the time was where I was in class and everybody had their books except me. All of these dreams relate back to fear. Fear of failure. Our subconscious mind is constantly letting us know that we are not fully prepared for an impending situation.

This fear of failure is what keeps us from trying and in turn, learning new things.

Too many of us blame outside influences on our failures, when in fact our failures were merely caused by a lack of preparation. It is this lack of preparation that is creating our fear of failure. It is our fear of failure that keeps us in our "comfort zone."

Fear has been described best as FALSE EVIDENCE APPEARING REAL. What if we didn't have any fear of failure?

What if we didn't have a "comfort zone"?

Would you be "uncomfortable" all the time? No. On the contrary, you would be more comfortable. Who doesn't want to be more comfortable? I know I do!

You were not born with a comfort zone. It is something you created.

As a child you just stared out into this wonderful new world around you and experienced every minute. You had to be taught by your parents, which things were dangerous. You are still being taught. It´s just that when you were three you were taught that touching a hot stove will burn you. Now you are being taught not to get burned by new relationships.

The difference is the teacher. Now the teacher is you. And the classroom is twenty-four hours a day, seven days a week! You have taught yourself to stay where you are safe from the danger of failure. Do you see what´s wrong with that? No growth! Without pushing yourself for more knowledge, more experiences, and more lessons, there will be no growth!

What happens when something stops growing? It starts dying. If you stop watering a plant, it doesn't just stay the same size, it starts dying. And so, will you!

We have grown up with the paradigm of the comfort zone. How many times have you heard that you need to step out of your comfort zone in order to grow?

But don't go too far…that's the danger zone!

So, we attach a bungee cord to our brain and stretch it out as far as it will go by experiencing things outside our comfort zone.

It has been said, "That which does not kill us makes us stronger," so we grow! And so does our comfort zone! Unfortunately, in this paradigm the zone of growth is temporary. The danger zone is still on the other side.

What if we changed the paradigm? You see, that's the beauty of this paradigm. It´s YOUR paradigm to change!

My comfort zone is a zone of no growth. A zone of no growth is a zone of death and decay! What I truly desire is balanced success, and I'm sure you do as well.

"The foundation stones for a balanced success are honesty, character, integrity, faith, love and loyalty."

The foundation of growth is learning, failing, new experiences, and succeeding. Remember, failure is an event, not a person.

As a recovering alcoholic, I find serenity in the fact that I am no longer in charge of what I could not change. But I also realize that I can prepare myself better and become better equipped to handle the things I cannot change.

For example, I can´t change the fact that the nail up ahead on the highway is going to give me a flat tire. What I can change is how I react to the circumstances. If I am un-prepared, I will find myself on the side of the road, frustrated and late for work! All of the motivational materials in the world are not going to change that fact.

"What we grow in the valley is what we eat on the mountain top."

In other words, the hard times (or valleys) is where we grow the experience and knowledge we will need later. So, having had multiple flat tires in the past and not wanting to ever be late for work, I have learned two things: leave 10 minutes early for work and make sure I have a good spare tire and jack!

I'm sure you've heard the expression "a lack of planning on your part does not constitute an emergency on my part!" Well, for me, having had a career in the US Coast Guard, a lack of planning on your part constitutes my job.

Thus, the motto of the US Coast Guard, Semper Paratus… Always Prepared!

The more you pursue honesty, character, integrity, love and loyalty, the better prepared you will be to embrace new opportunities and stay firmly in the growth zone! We need to form the good habit of learning something new every day. It doesn't have to be a quantum physics formula. It could be something as simple as a new word to improve our vocabulary. What we are doing is forming a good habit. The habit of learning. The habit of growing. If

we practice this habit every day, our subconscious mind will now switch its focus to encourage us to try new things and explore uncharted territory.

Suspend disbelief! Change your comfort zone paradigm and change your life! You were born to succeed and graced with a purpose!

Chapter Eight

WHAT IS REPEATED IS REWARDED

It was on a trip with my boys to watch them compete in the Mexican National Surfing Championships in Mazatlan that my big break came. We were staying at our sister resort. I was called to go see my boss in his office, and he explained to me that they needed to replace the current sales manager. He asked me if I wanted the job!

As a sales manager of a resort of that size, I was looking at making at least $250k a year! The boys and I agreed it was what I had been working for all those years and too good of an opportunity to pass up. They were at an age where they didn't want to move but it was just a short flight from Cabo and they could visit me all the time and surf.

Their mother wasn't as supportive of the idea and was concerned that I might fail. She decided to stay in Cabo. While all of her concerns were real fears to her, I had faith in my abilities. I had faith in my boss's judgment. I had faith that GOD had opened this door for me.

Two weeks later, I was on a plane by myself to Mazatlan. I lived at the resort for a month until I was able to rent my own place. I loved my new job! I had a team of some of the best people I have met to this day. I made some really good friends and we enjoyed our successes together. I was truly in my element and I was proud to have my own sales team at one of the highest rated five star resorts in the world. I looked forward to going to work each day and leading my morning meetings. I spent hours each week preparing sales training that would be both educational and motivational. I actually enjoyed the pressure of my boss breathing down my neck to perform. My work ethic and my ability to repeat positive behavior over the previous 13 years had brought me many rewards...I had this!

If changed behavior is the result of brokenness, then my brokenness was the beginning of my journey to living life successfully.

Chapter Nine

YOUR ENTHUSIASM IS CONTAGIOUS!

This is one of my favorite topics of training. Now, hopefully, anybody reading this book already appreciates the power of positive thinking.

Having a positive attitude can make a massive difference in every facet of your life and in turn, your performance.

There is actually a formula for performance.

You should always look at your life as a business. You own that business. Therefore, your success is determined by the performance of that business, and ultimately you are responsible for that performance.

The formula is simple:

$A \times E \times S = P$

Or

ATTITUDE X EFFORT X SKILL = PERFORMANCE

In your mind, picture a young man or woman who is entering the workplace for the first time. (Every business needs this entry level employee!)

He or she is happy to finally have a job after all of the knocking on doors and interviews and rejections. That person is going to show up for the first day of work excited and full of promise.

Why?

Well, they have a job! So, they have a good attitude. They want to get through that first day without getting fired so they put forward some effort. As of now, they have only the skills they brought with them.

$1 \times 1 \times 1 = 1$

At the end of that day their supervisor tells them, "You did a GREAT job today! We can´t wait to have you back tomorrow!"

So, encouraged, the next day they show up with an even better attitude. That leads them to putting in more effort, but the skill level is still the same. This increases their attitude and effort levels to a 2.

$2 \times 2 \times 1 = 4$

"Wow!" the boss says to them, "you've really got potential!"

Now, what do we do with the employee that shows potential? We TRAIN them, of course! So, with some basic training the skill level increases. With some basic training the skill level increases to a 2.

$2 \times 2 \times 2 = 8$

It is at this level of skill that most businesses stop training. They can get by pretty well with a factory full of eights. (Eighty percent of today's workforce measures an eight!)

But what about the guy you need to run the factory? Oh! That's the SELF- MOTIVATED employee! That's YOU!

You invest in yourself and you constantly raise your game.

You are committed to becoming the best you can be. The fact that you are reading a personal development book separates you from the masses! You watch motivational Podcasts and read self-help and skill-building books. You attend seminars and workshops. This is YOU! Because you understand this, you take your attitude, your activity, and your skill to a 3.

$3 \times 3 \times 3 = 27$

Now a 27 can get things done! A 27 can motivate others. A 27 can supervise others. But it takes a 64 to RUN the business!

$4 \times 4 \times 4 = 64$

So, what happens when a 64 is having a bad day?

I've always tried to maintain that level of 64 in all my affairs. Of course, it hasn't always worked out that way. In my Coast Guard days, I was a bit of a "discipline problem." You see, I'm classified as ADD in H.D.!

I was attached to the 378 ft. High Endurance Cutter Jarvis out of Honolulu, Hawaii. I was a Quartermaster (navigator). Now the "less fun" bunch on the ship got advanced in rate on a regular basis. You start out as a seaman recruit, advance to seaman, then to petty officer third class, second class, first class, etc. Well, let's just say I was a petty officer third class three times and leave it at that!

I did, however, have a great deal of time in the service and attained the experience and skill level that go with that assignment. I had just been advanced to "leading quartermaster of the watch." Now, on a ship underway in the middle of the ocean (yes, the Coast Guard DOES go into deep water!), you divide the bridge watches into four-hour sections. As the senior quartermaster, I had my choice and took the 4-8 watch, 4 o'clock in the morning until 8 o'clock in the morning.

It was great to wake up earlier than the rest of the sleeping crew and go out on deck to shoot the ship's position in relation to the stars and planets with my sextant. It was my job to plot the day's course based on those calculations in addition to the current, tides, wind, hull speed and set and drift. When all of my calculations had been made, I was free to watch the magnificent sunrise from the bridge wing.

Every morning, one of my duties was to inform the captain of all the information I had gathered during my watch. He would use that information to make critical decisions throughout the day.

The captain is the only person on the ship who is allowed to write in red ink. That way when you saw some instruction in red you knew it came directly from the captain. The captain always signed my log book at the end of my watch. One morning he used his red ink pen to write a little extra.

"Congratulations, Petty Officer Lowe. With experience comes knowledge. With knowledge comes promotion. With promotion comes responsibility, and with responsibility comes accountability. Be careful. Your enthusiasm is contagious." Captain Busik USCG

Why the sarcastic warning?

Well let´s look again at the formula for success.

$-4 \times 4 \times 4 = -64$

A highly trained, highly skilled employee with a BAD attitude can ruin a business. Or sink a ship!

Chapter Ten

OUTGROWING FEAR

Now that we have a basic understanding or description of our habits that have become character defects, we need to dig a little deeper and discover why we have them in the first place. We need to take a good look at the words we have listed as character defects, and try to figure out why we still hang on to them in our adult life.

Let's take a look at the second word on our list, jealousy.

The dictionary defines jealousy as a feeling of unhappiness and anger because someone has something or someone that you want.

Interestingly, I don't think there's anything wrong with wanting something or someone and being a little unhappy that we don't have it. This feeling of unhappiness is the motivation we need to take action to get the something or someone we want. The problem is, when we become angry and our jealousy of those that do have the something or someone we want turns into resentment.

Ahh, there's that word again... Resentment.

"Taking poison and waiting for the other guy to die!"

After a while, I got pretty used to being in Mazatlan on my own. The boys were 19 and 21 now and on their own in Cabo. I was making about $15k a month. I was surfing a lot. I spent a lot of time in town. I rented a fully furnished house on the marina with a dock behind it and access to a private pool. I bought a customized, 1964, F100 pick-up truck to cruise the malecon (boardwalk) with. I had a sweet set-up. I really thought I was doing and had everything I always wanted.

Things were going pretty well at work except for this one guy that I really didn´t care for. I´ve always tried to be a team player myself, and because of that I guess I just don´t have a lot of patience when it comes to the prima donna salesman who thinks he deserves more than everybody else and believes that the rules don't apply to him.

I had a particularly bad episode with this salesman one day and lost my patience. Webster defines patience as the capacity to accept or tolerate delay, trouble, or suffering without getting angry or upset. I was very angry and very upset and I let him know it in no uncertain terms!

Now the issue with this type of salesperson is that they have no problem going right over your head to YOUR boss. Remember, the normal rules of chain of command mean nothing to him!

I was told by my boss that it would be easier to replace a manager than a million-dollar salesman and that this was my first and last warning. If I had another episode, he would expect my letter of resignation.

Now, a few years ago I would have blamed the events that followed on that particular salesman. I would have spent years of my life with resentment towards this person. Sobriety has taught me to take responsibility for my life. A longtime friend and mentor of mine once told me to "name it…claim it…and get rid of it!"

When asked what he meant by that, he replied, "It all comes down to being accountable for your life. When something goes wrong, look for your part in it. Take full responsibility for the role YOU played. Make a sincere attempt to make any amends necessary if your part caused harm to anyone else. Now that you have cleaned up your side of the street, you need to take out the trash, so to speak. Don't let the event take up any more space in your thoughts. When your house is in order and uncluttered by all of garbage of the past, it becomes much easier to deal with the new pile of rubbish that just appeared."

At the time, I was sober and had been for 11 years, but as the months I spent alone went by I drifted pretty far from the pink cloud of good fuzzy feelings that followed me around when I was first enjoying life without the problems, alcohol created. Realizing we would never reconcile our differences, and that the boys were grown, the decision was made to file for a divorce.

That decision made my days a roller coaster of emotions. When you go to work with things like divorce and lawyers and settlements on your mind, you are definitely a (-) 64 employee!

Well, let me tell you, that prima donna salesman picked the right day to get under my skin! I knew it was about to get ugly, so I e-mailed the boss my letter of resignation and THEN proceeded to LET HIM HAVE IT!

I was fired immediately and my replacement was on a plane from Cabo San Lucas the next day. Luckily, they allowed me to stay on as a salesman. Wow, talk about screwing up! I was so far into my Danger Zone!

Between the divorce and losing my job, I was feeling all of the same feelings I had felt years earlier on that fateful Mother's Day. I wanted to run. I put all of my stuff into my car and got a room at a cheap motel.

The success I had achieved was so BAD I drank over it. Yep, 11 years of sobriety down the drain.

Alcoholism is a progressive disease. They say your mind remembers where you were when you quit drinking and puts you right back there, when you relapse. Well, all it took was two beers and I was ready to end it all over again! I have always believed God puts people in our lives for a reason. They become our Who. I'm sure Danea was. I met Danea shortly after moving to Mazatlan. She was going through a divorce as well. What I would come to understand and cherish over the next 10 years of our relationship would be the depth of her unconditional love. Not for me, but for herself and her vision of the life she wants to live and the people she has chosen to share it. When I met Danea, I was lost spiritually. I would suggest to anyone reading this, that the quickest way to succeed is to follow the path of those who have achieved what you define as success. Not only was she beautiful and in fantastic physical health, her personal sobriety program was strong and her self-image was contagious. I am so thankful that I have Danea in my life. That night, she definitely talked me off the ledge. By the grace of God, my relapse to drinking was very short-lived.

Let me set the scene...I could no longer afford the rent on my posh marina condo in Mazatlan. I had been staying at Danea's apartment. My self esteem was at an all time low and I really felt like I didn't deserve the wonderful relationship we were beginning to enjoy. After 11 years of sobriety, I packed everything I owned into my Jeep and went out specifically to get drunk.

When she came home and found all of my things were gone, she took action.

She kept calling me until I answered from the hotel room I had rented for the night. She talked to me until I fell asleep.

The next morning I went to work with my stuff in the car. I called My boss after work and he agreed to let me come back to Cabo. I grabbed my board out of my car to get in one last surf session in front of the hotel before I said goodbye to Mazatlan forever.

When I got out of the water to leave, Danea was waiting next to my car. I asked her what she was doing here and where her car was. She said she took a taxi, because the only way she was leaving was with me!

We moved back to Cabo together.

The problem was that I had been reversing the BE…Do…Have paradigm.

I thought if I had all the things I wanted, I could do all the things I wanted to do, and I would be happy. What I now realize is that in order to be a good salesperson, you must first be a good person. Be, the right kind of person, be happy, be loving and be caring. Be trustworthy and be loyal. When you start doing the next right thing from this place of being, you will immediately discover that what you are doing will manifest the things you've always wanted to "have."

So what, I had had a little slip. That's all. Nope! That´s not all…I had to do one of the toughest things a recovering alcoholic has to do, re-set my sobriety date. I had to start all over. True success requires rigorous honesty and persistent consistency. Remember that failure is an event, not a person. That puts everything in perspective.

I have experienced AMAZING spiritual, physical and financial growth during my "new sobriety." My goals and dreams are becoming my realities. It's my unconditional FAITH and belief that constant development of the foundation stones of success keeps me in the growth zone. When I stop caring, when I get lazy or do irresponsible things, I immediately begin to sink down toward the Danger Zone and the lifestyle that led to my brokenness. That knowledge is all the incentive I need to pursue growth daily.

Fear is faith in reverse.

The more you pursue honesty, character, integrity, love and loyalty, the better prepared you will be to embrace new opportunities and stay firmly in the growth zone.

Chapter Eleven

YOU + GOD = ENOUGH!

So how do we keep a positive outlook in the bad times? And there will be bad times!

The best tool I have in my toolbox is GRATITUDE!

Remembering "What we grow in the valley is what we eat on the mountain top," we must then acknowledge that the "God of the mountaintop is also the God of the Valley." Just thanking God for the things we count as good before we eat our Thanksgiving dinner isn't enough. We must maintain an attitude of gratitude for the gifts of experience and knowledge we are given in the bad times as well!

Adopt this affirmation: "My faith gives me the strength to look for the good in every situation."

Remember to use the visual of having to "prime the pump" in order to get water from the well. You have to put something in before you can get something out. Remember how important it is to guard what goes in.

That 'thing' we have to prime the pump with daily is gratitude. Every morning, set aside a few minutes to 'get familiar with' or meditate.

In this quite time think of the three most important things you are grateful for. My personal list always starts with my sobriety. I know that without that gift, nothing else would be possible. Repeat this ritual right before you go to bed. Science has shown us that as much as we try, it is impossible for our minds to multitask. When we fill our thoughts with feelings of gratitude, our brain blocks any other negative thoughts. It releases dopamine and serotonin, the two crucial neurotransmitters responsible for our emotions, and they make us feel 'good'. They enhance our mood immediately, making us feel happy from the inside. This seems like a great way to start and end any day, no matter what trials and tribulations the events of day may have produced.

The key is to direct our gratitude towards the one who graced you with the blessings in your life that you are grateful for. That one is God.

We all feel a certain sense of entitlement. We've put in the work. We feel that we deserve the appropriate level of respect and the authority that goes with it. At least, that's what our ego feels. Inevitably, it's our ego that gets upset and lashes out. When we finally come to the realization that in order to live life on life's terms, we must humble ourselves. Acceptance is the answer to all of our problems. If we accept that true success is only achieved when we are doing God's will, we must also accept that God can only do for us, what he can do through us. The achievements that we wave about and are so proud of, are not really ours at all. They are God's. Ever wonder why pride is listed first among the seven deadly sins? It's pride in ourselves as opposed to pride in what God has done through us. Be grateful for all of the experiences, gifts and talents that God has graced you with. Share these gifts with others freely, asking nothing in return as God did for you.

When you find yourself in one of life's many valleys, remain humble, give gratitude to God, trust your ability and use it to serve others. More importantly, trust God's plan for your ability.

I was told once, that a great way to grow your God given ability is to create an only practice. An only practice is something you've done to improve yourself that not many others would even attempt. I highly recommend that anyone wishing to really change their life, read Og Mandino's classic 'The Greatness Salesman in the World'. However, don't just read the book, that would only take a few days. Do what I did. I followed the instructions in the book. I took ten months and read each chapter three times a day for thirty days.

The book is a simple story of replacing bad habits with good ones. Remember, the only way to replace a habit is with another habit.

"The more bad habits you can replace with good ones, the more they become a pleasure to perform, and if it is a pleasure to perform, it is man´s nature to perform it often."

Og Mandino

"The fastest way to success is to replace bad habits with good habits."

Tom Ziglar

Chapter Twelve

WHY I AM

Today, I refuse to let my mind keep me from liking myself. I have changed my habit of negative self-talk to a habit of positive self-talk. One of my favorite parts of the Seminars I teach is the "I like me, because" exercise.

First, we write on the board a number of words that we use to describe successful people. Words like, passionate, goal oriented, driven, punctual, honest, etc. Next, each student takes a blank piece of paper and writes at the top, "I like (their own name) because…" and they have their neighbor tape it to their back. The whole class then spends about 10 minutes going around the room writing what they like about the person on each other's backs. The hardest part of this training is getting them to stop after 10 minutes! When we do finally get seated again, I ask a few members of the class to volunteer to read their list aloud.

Patty reads,

"I like Patty because she is an amazingly strong woman."

I then ask Patty to reword that statement as an affirmation. "I AM AN AMAZINGLY STRONG WOMAN!"

Doug reads,

"I like Doug because he is thoughtful and caring." Doug rewords his statement as an affirmation.

"I AM THOUGHTFUL AND CARING!"

We must realize our net worth will never grow until we have a firm image of our self-worth. The easiest way to boost our self-worth is to remember WHO we are and WHO's we are.

At the burning bush God said to Moses, "I AM WHO I AM. Thus, you shall say to the sons of Israel, 'I AM has sent me to you...This is My name forever!"

While there are over 100 names man has used for God in the Bible, I AM is the only name God actually told us to use.

"I Am" are the most powerful two words we can speak to ourselves.

When we affirm to our subconscious mind "I am successful, I am beautiful, I am strong, I am healthy" we are actually saying "God and I" are successful, beautiful, strong and healthy. With a strong self-image and faith in God we can do anything.

Soon everyone has taken what their classmates thought of them and turned them into empowering affirmations! I remind them to look at their new list of affirmations and repeat them from their heart daily.

Take it one step further. Positive affirmations are basically trying to convince our subconscious mind that we are successful, happy, rich etc. by repeating them over and over again and hoping that we are attracting these things into our lives. Problem is, our subconscious is not always buying in. It often quickly overrides the positive affirmation with…uh, no you're not!

Unfortunately, our subconscious is full of negativity. Unleash the hidden power of 'afforemations'.

If we truly want to do God's will and be successful, happy and rich, we sometimes have to override our monkey mind's negativity with positive "thoughts from our heart" Our monkey mind's habitat is a false world made up of mostly negative images from our past and based on that, mostly negative images of our future. Our heart only knows now. God speaks to us through our heart. If you find this to be true, instead of repeating the affirmation "I am happy and grateful" ten times a day, use afforemations, by simply asking yourself in silence, WHY am I happy and grateful? If you are truly doing the work, your heart will list for you, very quickly, all of the things you have to be happy and grateful for. This will immediately put you into the proper vibration to receive God's grace, and in turn, show you the 'next right thing' that will indeed make us successful, happy and rich!

You were BORN to SUCCEED and GRACED with a PURPOSE! The result of doing these exercises will be a much-improved self-image. Improving your self-image will increase your net worth. Increasing your net worth will give you the confidence you need to keep growing. When people are purposely growing, they approve of and like themselves more.

When you grow, you move AWAY from your danger zone and have no need for a comfort zone to hold you back!

Chapter Thirteen

THE GROWTH ZONE

Mountains and valleys, that´s life.

We learn, we grow…and if we´re smart about it, we take action!

"I the Lord search the heart and test the mind, to give every man according to his ways, according to the fruit of his deeds." Jeremiah 17:10

BE. DO. HAVE.

Thankfully, my boss made it very easy for me to return to Cabo.

Even though I had really let him down, our longtime friendship and our mutual respect kept that door open. One thing I have learned for sure over the years is to never burn my bridges. 25 years into our friendship, he truly is a trusted mentor and an important "Who" in my life.

He told me once you can never really go home. I believe this is true. While I was greeted with open arms and welcoming smiles, something had changed. I had done it all; the million-dollar dad, the loyal assistant, and now the manager who could have had it all! I felt the loss of respect.

Believing that's how my peers were thinking of me, affected my performance. Remember, your self-image creates your self-worth. You see, nobody really expected me to perform at my previous high levels of achievement, so I didn't. I ended the year with only $660k in volume. A far stretch from the $1 million plus 11 years in a row that had earned my advancements!

They were okay with the comfort zone I had slipped into, but I wasn't. I was bored. I wasn't growing, so I must have been dying! Well, I wasn't about to do that ever again.

As I mentioned earlier, I truly believe people are put into your life for a reason. For me, one of these people was someone who has helped me along my path of sobriety and in doing so become a pretty solid mentor of mine.

He was the sales director of another resort in town. A resort I had thought of as "the enemy" for the last fifteen years. He suggested that I might need to start all over again. Fresh, somewhere "my deeds, not my past accomplishments, would have to prove who I was."

Some of the best advice I've received is to always "go where you are celebrated, not tolerated."

I took a leap of faith. A big one!

We've all heard the saying, when one door closes another one opens! However sometimes the one that's trying to close is hitting us in the butt! We see the open door and we know opportunity is on the other side, but it's scary to take that step. Even though we're no longer growing, we are afraid to let the door close behind us. We have grown comfortable in that place of no growth. There is a saying, when you are no longer happy where you are working, and you start looking around at other opportunities that you are one foot out the door. A lot of us, end up staying right there for a very long time. We're not happy where we are but we are afraid of the unknown and the fear of losing what we had. When we are one foot out the door, we are neither here or there. If you are looking, you've already left! That still small voice inside you is telling you it's time to grow! Take the step! We were born to succeed. Success requires growth. Have faith in your ability. Have faith in that still small voice.

A lot of my friends thought I was nuts to leave a job of 15 years where I apparently could do no wrong, to work for a company that had a reputation for regularly firing people for not performing!

But they had another reputation as well. This company was dedicated to training their employees. This company was dedicated to serving the client.

Both of my passions, training and service, in one place! I had found a new home.

It was not easy. In fact, adjusting to my new job was the hardest thing I had ever done. Fifteen years of doing everything my way; fifteen years of exercising what had become bad habits; fifteen years of being "one of the best" on the team had set me in my ways. But this was a new team. I had to start from scratch. I thought my way was still better. Well, it wasn´t! After about three weeks of bucking the system with limited results I realized I need to make some changes.

It was just before Christmas and the sales director had called for a quarterly meeting of all three salesrooms. In this meeting of over 130 sales reps and management staff he discussed the company's goals for the following year. He put out a challenge of a $250 cash bonus to the salesperson that submitted the best personal goals for the year.

I have spent countless hours preaching the values of goal setting to my teams. I realized this challenge was the boost I needed, so I wrote out my goals. Following is what I wrote.

My goals for the next year

They have nothing to do with money.

I left a job and a company that I worked at for almost 15 years.

Eleven back-to-back million-dollar trophies, assistant management, and finally management.

I left in high season.

Why? I left to "re-invent" myself.

My goal for the next year is to learn a new system.

My goal for the next year is to learn to work with a new team.

My goal for the next year is to feel comfortable with the verbiage, styles and closing techniques that work here and lose the bad habits that have worked their way into my presentation over the years.

My goal for the next year is to develop an entirely new presentation, based on the new input from my team leaders and managers.

My goal for the next year is to become an integral member of the team.

I will work very hard to achieve these simple goals, rather than to be constantly after a high close percentage, or a set volume amount.

By achieving these goals in my first year, my success will manifest itself. By achieving these goals, my volume will manifest itself.

By achieving these goals, my closing percentage will manifest itself. By achieving these goals, my true potential will manifest itself.

I won the $250, but by committing to these goals and taking massive action towards the realization of these goals, I won a great deal more.

Many times, in our lives we feel that we have not accomplished everything we set out to do. We feel there are plans that we never finished, and projects that we should've started a long time ago. These feelings can cause us to get frustrated and make rash decisions. We get all caught up in trying to decide what to do next. It is during these times that it is most important to find a place where we can just stay still. We need quiet, introspective time where we can listen to our heart. While our conscious monkey mind is holding a kangaroo court and presenting us with a million reasons why we shouldn't act on our heart's impulses, we need to yield and listen to that still, small voice that is trying also to present its case. Once we have given our heart the opportunity to express itself, and we truly listen...we will intuitively know what step to take to do the next right thing.

In Bob Beaudine's second book, *2 Chairs: The Secret That Changes Everything,* we are encouraged to sit down with God every morning and ask three crucially disruptive questions---Does he know your situation? Is this too hard for him? Does he have a good plan? As we listen to that still small voice, we will discover the answers, and be well equipped to walk courageously and faithfully to the other side of any crisis. My 2 Chairs time has become my most important and fulfilling daily ritual.

As the Cowardly Lion wailed in the Wizard of Oz, "What have they got that I ain't got? COURAGE!" In order for us to continually grow spiritually and to stay out of our danger zone, we must have courage. Not courage in the hero sense of the word, but courage to embrace humility. It takes courage to realize that we don't always make the right decisions. It takes courage to admit when we are wrong. It takes courage to acknowledge our bad habits. Most of all, it takes courage to have faith in God's plan for our success. When we truly give our life over to the care of God and seek to only do his will, we will find the courage and guidance to do the next right thing.

Chapter Fourteen

SUSPEND DISBELIEF

"The best part of writing an autobiography is doing the research."

I was raised by my mother and father in a very religious Jewish family. In Sunday school we studied the Bible. That is, OUR bible, the Old Testament. As I grew older and wandered off into the world on my own it was suggested to me by my older brother that there was more out there…a lot more!

The one thing I have learned and have been sharing with you up to this point is the undeniable power of faith in our lives. It´s what gets us through the hard times and pushes us even further in the good times.

I was researching the word "faith" on the Internet and came upon an amazing discovery. In the Old Testament the word faith only appears 18 times while it appears 246 times in the New Testament.

I sent a text to Tom Ziglar to ask him what he made of my discovery. This was his reply:

"Not sure how relevant the word count of faith is, but I think I can give you perhaps why it is so different from Old to New Testament. The

Old Testament is about living under God's Law, the rules to life and how to honor God. Man was sinful and his responsibility was to obey God's law and offer blood sacrifices as atonement.

"The New Testament is about grace. Salvation is a gift of God. Jesus died for our sins as a perfect sacrifice to atone for our sins. By faith we accept Christ's sacrifice. It is a free gift, something we can only accept and not earn. It takes faith to do this and that is why faith is mentioned so much more in the New Testament than the Old Testament. The Old Testament was about working your way into heaven. This concept of grace is what makes Christianity so different from every other religion. Hope this helps."

I then asked Tom if it is safe to say that faith and grace go and in hand.

(The word grace appears in the Old Testament 4 times and 118 times in the New Testament.)

Tom´s reply:

"Yes, from the Christian perspective. One of the challenges of people is we try and do everything without God, thinking we have all of the answers. Our pride gets in the way. Once we realize there is nothing, we can do to earn God's favor, that it is a gift, not as a result of our works, but Christ's sacrifice, then we have to swallow our pride and accept His grace - and it takes faith to do this. So yes, they do go hand in hand."

Tom also pointed out to me that the Old Testament is filled with stories of grace. Abraham sacrificing his son took faith and then God substituted the ram to take his place - grace.

How many times have you said to yourself, There, but for the GRACE of GOD go I? As a recovering alcoholic, I say it 10 or 12 times a day!

It is often expressed in AA meetings that when an alcoholic comes to the realization that he is powerless over alcohol and turns his will and his life over to the care of GOD (as he or she sees him), then and only then can the process of recovery begin. Many people say they felt like they called GOD on the phone one day and GOD replied I've been on the other end of the line the whole time…I was just waiting for you to pick up!

When you truly come to the realization that YOU are NOT in charge of the universe, then and only then can you begin to look toward God for His direction.

Zig Ziglar said, "Success is not measured by what you do compared to what others do, it is measured by what you do with the ability GOD gave you."

Does that mean I don't have to work?

On the contrary, we live in a world that requires money. Money keeps a roof over our head and food in our mouth.

Remember, we are comprised of mind, body and soul. We must feed the mind and the soul as well as our physical body. The only way to truly make the most out of the gifts we have been given is to continually nourish all three.

Chapter Fifteen

A NAVIGATOR'S TOOLS

A good navigator would never sail without a chart. He would also never leave the dock without telling others of his destination and route. It's so very important to know where it is you want to be and develop a secure route to get there. In a company, this chart would be called a mission statement.

Every company should have a well-defined mission statement that lets everybody who works for the company know why the company exists, and where the company wants to be. It is also imperative that the company knows exactly the course needed to get there. As an employee, it is equally important that our values and principles lineup with those of the company we work for. When those of the company and the employees, lineup, it truly benefits the clients that they serve. In our personal lives this mission statement is known as our vision, purpose and goals. As with any successful company, it is important that our values and principles lineup with God's plan for us. I highly encourage everyone reading this to take the time and effort required to define your personal mission statement. Having this as a reference point will motivate us, encourage us and hold us accountable.

Vision - **BE.**   Purpose - **DO.** Goals - **HAVE.**

> *"When you define success,*
> *you will find your purpose."*
>
> *Carey Lowe*

Here's my Vision, Purpose and Goals:

MY VISION

I was born to succeed! I have a burning desire to succeed! My vision of success is to lead by example and to loyally follow and seek guidance from those that have been chosen to lead me. My vision of success is to be sought after to motivate, train and mentor those who seek my success.

MY PURPOSE

I was graced with a purpose! My purpose is to do God's will. God's will for me is to be successful and create a living legacy. God's will for me to be an honest loving father to my sons and a faithful loving partner to Danea. I wake every morning with God's grace and he has chosen me to be a leader. It is my purpose to lead with honesty, character, integrity, faith, love and loyalty driven by passion, conviction, gratitude and a true concern for others.

MY GOALS

As an honest and loving man, I have nothing but serenity in my life. I hold my head up and my sons are as proud of me as I am of them. I remain madly in love with Danea as we travel the world together. My success has earned me respect. I have built a proud and financially solid legacy by helping other people achieve their dreams. I am happy and content. My faith is unwavering. I continue to seek guidance and am learning and growing daily. I remain grateful for all of the blessings as well as the challenges that are placed in my path. I am doing God's will.

I review this navigational chart often and make sure to make any needed corrections to the course I am on as quickly as possible. I have faith that GOD´S grace will shine upon me. I ask for his guidance in all I do. Then I do the work!

Faith without works is dead. James 2:14-26

Chapter Sixteen

STAY ON COURSE

As mentioned in an earlier chapter, I set out on an "only practice," to read all ten of Og Mandino´s scrolls three times a day as prescribed for 30 days. I was to find out that this required an amazing amount of self-discipline. As the days turned into weeks, and the weeks into months, I was replacing many of the bad habits I had accumulated over my lifetime with good, productive habits.

I was experiencing extraordinary growth and my sales numbers were doubling.

While attending a one-day seminar on growth and goals, I was asked to "put it out there." I firmly believe in this principle.

Shout your goals from the mountaintops! Let everyone hear them. Let the universe hear them!

We were told to write in our journal, "Make it happen, take action now!" We then were asked to list six things we would love in our life.

These were my six:

1) I would love an extraordinary life.
2) I would love to be a trainer for the Ziglar group.

3) I would love for my relationship with Danea to grow.

4) I would love to be fit enough to tackle any physical challenge I encounter.

5) I would love the wonderful relationship with my sons to grow even stronger through the years to come.

6) I would love to be considered a leader because I motivate others to seek extraordinary growth.

We then were asked to turn these into affirmations of what we want by imagining the word "I AM" in the place of "I would" and then to sign and date it.

That day, the same mentor who suggested it was time for me to change jobs was sitting in on the training and he signed it as well adding, "This or something even better!"

Now, I´m going to admit something here, I really like Facebook! I have well over 5000 friends and have found it to be the easiest way to stay connected. Please reach out to me. I really hate e-mailing, and quite frankly, I like all the cute pictures of puppies and kittens!

One day about three months after taking that seminar, I was reading a post from Bob Beaudine on his "The Power of Who" page, and noticed a response from Tom Ziglar about a Legacy Certification Course they were going to offer for the first time.

When I went to my first A school in the U.S. Coast Guard at age 21, I was introduced to Zig Ziglar's philosophies of training and living through audiotapes of his book "I'll see you at the Top!" Since then I have read and studied the habits of and listened to the advice of many motivational speakers and trainers. Over 40 years later, I can still look to that book, as one of the most personally inspirational and motivational ever written.

As the genius, Christopher Langan is quoted in Malcolm Gladwell's best seller Outliers, "I always find the closer you get to the original source, the better off you are."

I did some further investigation and discovered that it was to be offered only to a very small group of qualified applicants, and it would be held at the Ziglar Corporate offices in Plano, Texas.

Wow! What an opportunity. I decided to go for it! All they could say was no! (I was pretty sure that's exactly what they were going to say!) I called their office and asked them to send me an application via e-mail. They were very surprised to hear that I lived in Cabo San Lucas, Mexico, but said they would send me the forms to fill out, but not to get my hopes up.

First, I had to pass a background check. Then someone would review my application (all twenty pages of it!) and make the determination if I qualified for a final follow-up phone interview. Even if I was accepted, and paid the fee for the course, there was no guarantee of passing the course.

So, I filled out the application, sent it in…and waited, and waited.

After a while I had begun to think that having lived in Mexico for 22 years, I couldn't pass the background check. Or maybe the fact I had joined the Coast Guard and had no formal college education was the problem.

Whatever it was they weren't getting back to me. One of my closest friends even asked me, "why would they pick you?" The class was scheduled to start on March 30th and it was already March 25th. Well, stay focused on the things you are doing and don´t worry about the things that are out of your control, right? Right!

On a random date 10 months earlier, I set out on a journey to have a better life by committing to reading the ancient scrolls of "The Greatest Salesman in the World" three times a day for 30 days. I finished the last scroll on May 29th.

They say coincidence is God's way of staying anonymous. Remember, what is repeated is rewarded.

On the morning of May 30th, I was in Plano, Texas, shaking Tom Ziglar´s hand.

Chapter Seventeen

THE TEN COMMITMENTS

One of my duties in the Coast Guard was to update the charts. Buoy markers are moved, lighthouses are de-commissioned, etc. In other words, the world around you changes. Unless the charts you are using are current and up-to- date, they could prove to be a liability rather than an asset.

I believe the best way to navigate your life away from your danger zone and into the faith zone is to have an updated set of charts to get you there.

Therefore, we all need to re-evaluate or update our goals on a regular basis. Your course can be altered by your commitments.

We all set goals, but what commitments have we also made? Do our goals and commitments line up? Are we really prepared to commit to the goals we have set?

A pig and a chicken were out for a walk one day when they happened across a very sad-looking group of human beings. "Gee," said the pig, "I wonder what's wrong with them?" "I don't know," said the chicken. "But I wonder if they might be hungry. Let's cheer them up! Let's make them a bacon and egg breakfast!" The pig paused for a moment. "Hey," he said. "I'm not so sure I like that idea. For you it's a nice goal, but for me it's a commitment!"

We need to determine what it is we REALLY want. My suggestion before you get to work on setting your goals is first get to work on setting your commitments.

Zig Ziglar put it this way… "The chief cause of failure and unhappiness is trading what you want most for what you want right now."

Come up with a list of the commitments you have already made, for example;

1. FAMILY
2. WORK
3. RELATIONSHIP
4. FINANCIAL
5. CHURCH (community)

Now make a list of your immediate goals. (for example)

1. Take a trip
2. Stop drinking
3. Find a better job
4. Buy a new truck
5. Save money
7. Buy a house
9. Get out of debt
10. Lose 20 pounds

Now, put your goals to this test:

Do all of these goals work together with your commitments? Are your goals morally right and fair to everyone concerned? Are your goals consistent with your other goals?

Can you emotionally commit to finish these goals? Can you "see" yourself finishing these goals?

Keep working this list until you have come up with ten goals that you are willing to commit to!

These ten goals are now your TEN COMMITMENTS!

Here´s some great advice I was given. If you find that you are being distracted from a commitment you have made by a new or distracting goal, make that commitment an affirmation. For example;

"I commit to being the BEST, MOST ENERGETIC, MOTIVATED, (your job here) for thirty consecutive days. I only see the good in every situation."

Keep track of your progress. If you have a bad attitude day on day six, you MUST start over on that affirmation!

Chapter Eighteen

THE TOOLBOX

About 20 years ago, I was given a beautiful, 4 drawer tool box as a Father's Day present. Now, any dad reading this knows the true feeling of joy in receiving a gift like this that he can really use! Over the years, that empty tool box became full. Full of tools...and memories. I made sure never to buy a junky tool. I knew that they didn't last. I was taught by my father, that tools were an investment. I was also taught the importance of having the 'right tool for the job'. My dad showed me that while a pair of pliers will loosen or tighten the nut on a battery cable connection, it will also inevitably, strip the nut and eventually render it useless. The proper tool is a socket wrench.

More specifically, a 10mm wrench or socket, as most car battery cables have this size nut attached. As the years past, that toolbox was filled with precisely the right tool for the job. Tools that my boys and I needed for the job at hand. It's larger cabinet became home to the Circular saw we used to build the skateboard ramp in our backyard. It's lower drawer separated the metric T-wrenches that became incredibly valuable as the boys raced motocross. We took that toolbox to every race. When I moved to Mazatlan to assume my new management position, I left everything behind in Los Cabos. Once divorced, I never returned for the toolbox. Many times, I thought of sending for it. After all, I bought those tools. I owned them. Nobody had any right to them except me. Even though I no longer really needed them, I felt I had the exclusive right to them. Years went by. Both my ex-wife and I moved many times. I lost track of the tool box, and assumed the tools had been sold off or lost. Recently, I have been blessed with grandchildren. On a visit to Los Cabos, my oldest son Kane gave me a tour of his new workshop. Kane has become a respected surf and skimboard craftsman. His young son was holding his hand as we walked and talked. He explained the processes and specific tools he used to create his custom boards. I was truly impressed. He got a phone call and left me to wander around for a few minutes. There, in the corner of his workshop, sat the toolbox. I opened a few drawers. Every tool was there, and in perfect working order. Kane explained to me later that he made sure to keep the toolbox when I left. The fact that he still had it and used it daily, taught me something more valuable. The toolbox and the tools in it were never mine. They were a legacy of work ethic and instruction intended to be passed down, and to be used by the ones we care about. I would love to think this toolbox will one day be sitting in one of my grandchildren's garage. The tools that get passed down from generation to generation are not always mechanical. The professional and spiritual advice we receive from our mentors should be considered valuable tools as well. We then, as my dad did for me, have a responsibility to show those we care for, how to use them and the importance of passing them on.

One day, listening to Tom Ziglar train, I let him know that I really liked something he said, and jokingly told him that I was going to steal it for my training. He said if I did, I would have stolen it twice! Nothing in this, or any other motivational book is truly original. Our responsibility, is to learn from others and in turn, pass that knowledge on to those we care about. Tom explained, "it's the sin of the desert to know where the water is, and not share it with those in need."

Here's a few valuable tools that have been passed on to me over the years...

As a manager, I often ask sales people (who didn't get a sale), if you got that same couple tomorrow what would you do differently? It has been said that we are all salesmen, no matter what our actual profession. This analysis then, as simple as it may sound, is the best way for anyone to learn from your experience. What one little thing could we have done differently or said differently that might've made a positive difference? The key then is to put that new element into action. We've all heard the saying that insanity is doing the same thing over and over again and expecting different results. So, if tomorrow we are faced with the exact same adversity or problems that we encountered today what would we do differently? Don't wait for tomorrow when we're faced with them. Think about them now.

Come up with a plan now, and take action now! It is possible to change our life. It is possible to achieve success...One day at a time, one choice at a time!

100% ACCOUNTABILITY / 0 EXCUSES!!!

In the military, there is only one acceptable answer for not performing an assigned task.

NO EXCUSE, SIR!

The point is... when we make excuses, we give away our power to improve. When we are 100% accountable it means WE are 100% in control. And that's a glorious thing. When we can admit that when there's a problem, we are the problem. It also means WE are the solution!

100% accountability. No finger pointing EVER!

INCREASE OUR 'ABILITY'!!'

Acceptability -

The act of taking or receiving something offered that we cannot change.

Flexibility - what	The willingness to change or compromise we can.
Responsibility -	The ability or authority to act or decide on our own, without supervision.
Accountability -	Being expected to (or required to) ACCOUNT for our actions!

Are you ready to hold yourself accountable? With ZERO excuses? That is, accepting the incredible power that comes with knowing if there is a problem, you are the problem and therefore you are the solution!

Take the 30-day 100/0 challenge!

"I commit to being the best I can be for the next 30 consecutive days."
" I will see only the good in every situation!"

> *"If you see someone without a smile,*
> *give them one of yours."*
>
> *Zig Ziglar*

Rabbi Lapin teaches us that we should think of money as "certificates of appreciation". We earned that money because somebody appreciated the work we did. When we buy something, we feel that the item we're buying had enough value for us to part with our certificates. So, the question we all want answered is how do we get more certificates of appreciation? The answer is simple...be appreciated more! What are we bringing to our work place that makes everybody there appreciate our presence? Promotions and raises are given to those who have earned them. If we are only giving the bare minimum, we will only be appreciated minimally. If we give great value we will be rewarded with great appreciation. The easiest thing of value for us to give and the most appreciated thing we have is our smile...give away your smile sincerely and watch your certificates of appreciation multiply!

LOOKING THROUGH SPIRITUAL EYES

"Faith is the assurance of things hoped for, the conviction of things not seen..."

Sometimes the world seems to just not make any sense. We need to not only maintain our faith in times like these, we need to strengthen it. It's at times like these that we need to change perspective. How we look at the world around us. We need to step back and look at the world through spiritual eyes. Spiritual eyes see the world stripped clear of politics, race, religion and any of the other filters we might be placing in front of us. Spiritual eyes seek to understand how everything is a part of everything, and that everything happens for a purpose. Spiritual eyes recognize the beauty in even the smallest thing. Spiritual eyes do not see good or bad. Spiritual eyes realize that everything has a season. Spiritual eyes see with gratitude. Spiritual eyes look for the good in every situation. Spiritual eyes are happy even when we feel sad, knowing that God's plan is much larger than we can comprehend.

Spiritual eyes help others who cannot find their way to see clearly. When we practice looking at the world through spiritual eyes, we will feel our faith strengthen and our hope restored.

Chapter Nineteen

LEARNING THE HARD WAY

Over the years, I've been repeatedly told that I can "either do this the easy way...or the hard way!" For some reason, I seem to always pick the hard way. I guess it comes back to mountains and valleys. The most valuable lessons are the ones I've learn in life's valleys.

In writing this book, I came to a mind blowing realization regarding finances. My finances. I'm not really sure how much value I actually place on the Zodiac, but I'm a Libra. The scales. The scales that are apparently never balanced. I seek balance in everything and everyone around me, but seldom experience it in my own life. As a motivational speaker and coach, I've spent a great deal of time stressing the value of one's self image. I've even gone so far as to coin the phrase "Your self-worth determines your net worth!" Writing a book can and should be very introspective. The disruptive question I must dig deep and ask myself then, is that over the 32 years of my successful sales career, having made huge sums of money, why haven't I saved huge sums of money and secured a financial future for myself and the ones I so dearly care about?

The answer, I've discovered comes back to self image. The day I got out of the Coast Guard with a disability discharge for a back injury,

I was told that I would receive a monthly check from the Veterans administration. Thirty two years later, I still receive that monthly deposit. Interesting though, I've never kept the money. I really never felt I deserved it. When I was asked to fill out some final forms, I looked across the desk at the Vietnam Vet in charge of the office who had both of his legs and one arm blown off. I've compared my minor discomfort to his ever since. The point I'm making, is that even though no one else would argue that I had definitely earned the money after 10 years of active duty, my self image kept me from keeping it and using it.

As a strictly commission salesman, I put up a front that I am not bothered by the daily rejection I must endure.

I always try to remember that failure is an event, not a person. A tool I was given and use daily has always been, SW-SW-SW-N! Some will, some won't, so what, Next! While this tool helps me clear my mind temporarily, my negative self-image that has been created over years of not doing the next right thing, slips back into control and my monkey mind steps in and eventually takes over. You'll remember me saying that I wasn't the most popular kid in the class back in 1974. As a matter of fact, I was one of the least. Trying to break into the cool surfer's clique, only seemed to make me less popular. Those memories still have a strong place in my negative self image bank. My brother and sister had already graduated high school and were experiencing college life on their own. At 13, my parents and I moved from the suburban bubble of Thousand Oaks to the bustling Navy town of San Diego. We actually lived on a houseboat. My mother was the editor of the Miramar Navy base newspaper. During the Vietnam conflict, Miramar was known as 'Fightertown' and was home to Top Gun. I immersed myself in all things navy and nautical. I took sailing lessons and got a job at the sailing school. I learned to scuba dive and cleaned boat bottoms in the marina. I really had a great time before and after school. It was from 8am until 3pm that I had a problem. I would wear my navy blue pea coat to school while the cool kids wore plaid Pendleton's. My hippy looking bell bottoms were a stark contrast to the blue Levi corduroys the surfers wore. In Thousand Oaks, I had embraced the rock music rebellion of the early seventies. In conservative 1970's Point Loma, I stood out like a sore thumb. I quickly found myself hanging out with other misfits. We would meet in the alley every morning and smoke pot. We skateboarded and surfed only with each other, making sure to keep away from the cool kids that seemed to always want to pick a fight. By 8th grade I had a reputation as a stoner. To make matters worse, one day an older guy showed up selling pills. A few of us bought some and took them before class. They turned out to be baking powder laced with strychnine. I passed out during gym class. I was lucky. One of the other kids died. I was suspended for drug use and carried that reputation with me into high school. I spent the next 3 years dodging insults and punches. My parents even had me change high schools hoping it would help. Unfortunately the new school was very lax in discipline and I spent most of my days skateboarding and surfing. I got pretty good at both. By the time I was seventeen and feeling that I would never fit in, I dropped out of high school and hitch-hiked to Santa Barbara. My older brother had established himself there and his introduction was all I needed to gain instant rapport. I re- invented myself. Nobody there knew the old me. To them, I was a really good surfer and skateboarder. I got on a surf team and a skateboard team. I finally returned to San Diego with hair down to my shoulders and a newfound confidence. I felt like the guy in the Eagle's hit 'New kid in town'! I look back now and see that the desire to be cool had created a lot of problems, but being treated as someone cool brought great rewards. I worked those rewards as hard as I could until they eventually fizzled out. One day, broke and partied out, I found myself skateboarding home from who knows where. I saw a Coast Guard recruitment office and went inside. Either that recruiter was really good or it was just God's way of staying anonymous, but I enlisted that day and consider that choice to be one of the best I've ever made. The deserved respect I experienced wearing my Coast Guard uniform and truly making a difference gave me a ten year respite from these old feelings of poor self worth. But once discharged, I had to find my way again on my own. The world of sales was a perfect solution. Turns out, as long as I was selling, I was a god! I could do no wrong. I could do all the drugs I wanted! I could come to work everyday with a hangover! As long as I was a top seller, everyone wanted to be around me. They sought out my advice and mentoring. The problem is, my popularity was and always felt temporary. I became attached to the sale as a measure of my success. The sale had become a powerfully addicting drug and my self image became determined by whether or not I got that sale. I soon learned that I could brush off the loss of one sale and just go get another one. There will always be another one.

This gave me a superhuman power. My sales skills made it feel like all I was doing was shaking a tree and money fell out. Lots of it. I had as little respect for the money as I did for myself. I spent most of it buying my kids toys so that they would think I was a cool dad. I spent the rest of it on cocaine and alcohol to mask the fact that inside, I really didn't believe I was. I alwayscknew that when I eventually ran out of money, all I had to do was 'shake the tree a little harder'. The money would appear, but very quickly it would just once again burn a hole in my pocket. The problem is, I'm not superhuman. In fact I'm very human. Because of that fact, my deep rooted negative self image, was telling me once again, that I didn't really deserve the money I had made so

I spent it as fast as I could get it. I've always been impressed by my friends who have been able to save money. As a salesperson who has put a lot of time and effort into the sales process, I've never really had a problem making money. I definitely never had a problem spending it. I have however, had a heck of a time hanging on to it. Until recently, I never knew why. It actually comes down to self image. Our own self image. As a salesperson, we are taught to become actors. We mirror and match our clients to get the deal. We create a character and play the role perfectly. Here's the problem. That character is the one making the money. That character is also the one spending the money. That character is not real. The things we end up spending our money on are not real either. They most often are things that support the lifestyle of the character we have created. They are things that boost the ego of an imaginary creation. The ability to hide behind this ego, is one of the reasons being a salesperson can become so addicting. When we are forced to take off the mask, we often find that we really don't like the person behind it. The person behind the mask doesn't feel worthy of the money the actor earned. The person behind the mask finds ways to spend the money as fast as possible. In order to increase our net worth, we need to increase our self worth. We need to spend more time working on the real person behind the mask

This has undoubtedly been the greatest personal reward of my new season of sobriety and spiritual growth. The more time I spend figuring out who I really am and more importantly why I am, the more my positive self image grows. The more I truly like the person I'm becoming, the more secure I grow financially as well. It helps to have a positive role model. As I shared with you in a previous chapter, one of the things I most admire about Danea is her unconditional love for herself. She will not allow her monkey mind to convince her that she deserves anything less than all of the happiness and prosperity this life has to offer her. You see, as opposed to me growing up in San Diego with a silver spoon in my mouth, Danea grew up in Mexico sharing a bed with her 5 brothers and sisters. Her desire to achieve more in life comes from a much deeper place. She has worked very hard to overcome any and all obstacles placed in her path by taking on a constant position of being an immediate problem solver. She takes positive action to keep moving and keep growing. Danea definitely does not have a comfort zone! She has taught me by example that as long as I continue to grow, as long as I continue to do the next right thing and as long as I love myself first, I can have anything I want, and more importantly...deserve to keep it.

Chapter Twenty

THE FAITH ZONE

So, what is that one, character defect? I like to share a lot about the need for growth. What I don't share very often is the inner turmoil I experience myself with it. Having committed this period of my life to a season of growth, I must constantly struggle with the enemy's desire for the opposite. For me, (and I'm guessing most of us) that enemy is dressed as my EGO. When our ego steps into the equation it tells us, we're fine the way we are. We don't need to listen to advice. We shouldn't have to do this much work to get what we truly desire. Well...our EGO is not our AMIGO! Our ego's voice is coming from our mind and our mind is full of negative thoughts and false perceptions.

That still small voice that is telling us the battle is worth it, is coming from our heart. Follow your heart. The obstacles in front of us were placed there for a reason. Embrace every one of them. Grow from them. Enjoy the work. Enjoy the season. Have faith in your ability.

I was asked to get up in front of the class on my very first day at Ziglar and give a five-minute presentation about myself.

Some of my classmates confessed later that that was the hardest thing they ever had to do. They didn't like stepping out of their "comfort zone" like that in front of perfect strangers.

For me, it was a perfectly enjoyable experience!

Six months earlier, at a mindset workshop, I was introduced to the concept of a burning ceremony.

I was asked to take some time and think of the one thing I would like to eliminate from my life. Something, that if it didn't exist at all, would help me achieve my ultimate goals.

I thought hard for a few minutes and then it came to me. We were asked to write the thing down on a piece of paper and to fold it up so no one could see it.

We were then told that the class was over and to exit the room slowly in a single file line, keeping the picture of the thing we had written clear in our mind. As I left the room and went outside, I saw there was a steel pot that had a wood fire burning in it. I was instructed to place my paper note into the burning pot.

As I watched my paper burn, I started to cry and then to feel a huge amount of hope, or what I now know to be GOD'S grace. What I had written on that paper was, COMFORT ZONE.

It was gone; gone forever.

I could never run back to it. I could never hide behind it. I no longer had a comfort zone!

Ready?

Step out of your comfort zone.

Now look back at it differently. That is what is called a paradigm shift; the simple act of looking at something differently.

Look back at your comfort zone as a place of zero growth. A place of death and decay, a place you want no part of. Your comfort zone has now become your danger zone, a place to stay away from. You no longer have a comfort zone!

Now look ahead. Nothing but opportunity!

From this moment forward, make this affirmation your mantra, I CAN!

GOD'S WILL! I'M POSITIVE!

The opportunity may come in different forms.

It may have to be sown in the valley before you can reap it on the mountaintop, but reap it you surely will because you are now in the FAITH ZONE!

Your FAITH, that was created by blood, sweat and tears.

Your FAITH, that as long as you stay out of the danger zone you will continue to learn.

Your FAITH, that as long as you continue to learn you will continue to grow.

Your FAITH, that GOD has graced you with gifts you cannot earn, but only need to accept!

Your FAITH, that you were BORN to WIN! Your FAITH, that you have PLANNED to WIN!

Your FAITH, that you have PREPARED to WIN, and the FAITH that GOD EXPECTS YOU TO WIN!"

For it is by grace you have been saved, through faith--and this is not from yourselves, it is the gift of God.

Chapter Twenty-One

TURN AT THE NEXT RIGHT THING… PROCEED TO GOAL!

So what does it mean, to do the next right thing? How do we know what it is, and more importantly…if it's the right time to do it? If the feeling is coming from your heart. JUST DO IT! That's the best advice I can give. Just do it! Do what? Take action. Some action. Any action. Move! The key is to not get tangled up in the paralysis of analysis. I've always loved the quote, "when you come to a fork in the road, take it!" It may not be the road that leads us to our ultimate goal…but it will get us closer. Why? Because we will be able to see a little further forward, and just as important, a little further back.

Standing still when our gut is telling us to move is a reaction produced by fear. False Evidence Appearing Real. Have faith in GOD's plan for us to succeed. Listen to your heart for guidance and then send that message to your mind to take MASSIVE ACTION NOW!

"Abandon yourself to God as you understand God. Admit your faults to Him and to your fellows. Clear away the wreckage of your past. Give freely of what you find and join us. We shall be with you in the Fellowship of the Spirit, and you will surely meet some of us as you trudge the Road of Happy Destiny."

May God bless you and keep you - until then." (Pg. 164, AA)

…Just keep paddling.

ZIGLAR LEGACY TRAINING AND COACHING

My story is not unique, but my ability to share my story with others is. From the moment I entered the world of sales, I found that my charismatic attitude would provide my family with an easy income. What I would learn the hard way, is that it takes more than charisma to succeed! My personal experiences before and after hitting rock bottom combined with my passion to help others succeed has equipped me with a spiritual toolbox that can get me through any situation. It is this toolbox that I now share with others. It's not enough to become a good salesperson and enjoy the benefits of success.

What is more important is learning how to live life on life's terms... when

you're not selling. As a Ziglar Legacy Certified Professional I have made a personal commitment to continue teaching the Ziglar Legacy. I have made it my personal and professional mission to promote the Ziglar Legacy as the most effective, balanced, and proven system for achieving true success in life. It is my purpose and burning desire to help others achieve extraordinary success, create significance and leave a legacy that will ripple through eternity. For more information regarding training or coaching visit me at www.careylowe.com

"You can have everything you want in life, as long as you help enough other people get what they want in life. ".
Zig Ziglar

"You were BORN to SUCCEED and GRACED with a PURPOSE!"
Carey Lowe